√ 7.50
B & T

Coleman

BOOKS BY JACKSON LEE ICE
published by The Westminster Press

SCHWEITZER: PROPHET OF RADICAL THEOLOGY

THE DEATH OF GOD DEBATE (Edited in collaboration
with John J. Carey)

SCHWEITZER: PROPHET
OF RADICAL THEOLOGY

SCHWEITZER: PROPHET OF RADICAL THEOLOGY

By
Jackson Lee Ice

THE WESTMINSTER PRESS
Philadelphia

ISBN 0–664–20906–8

LIBRARY OF CONGRESS CATALOG CARD NO. 74–141991

4 -9- 74

BOOK DESIGN BY
DOROTHY ALDEN SMITH

Published by The Westminster Press ®
Philadelphia, Pennsylvania

PRINTED IN THE UNITED STATES OF AMERICA

To my wife, Susan

Contents

Contents

Preface

THIS SPACE, traditionally reserved for the author's acknowledgments of services rendered, should contain first the name of Albert Schweitzer, whose life and work have focused into meaningfulness the inert lives of thousands and presaged the "new" works of unconventional thinkers now dominating the theological scene. It secondly should note the Radical theologians, who by their intensive efforts to clarify, free, and infuse with fresh meaning the religious concepts for our time, have unleashed a revolution emitting a positive and permanent impact to be only dimly evaluated from this temporal vantage point. Without the unique achievements of these men, no book such as this one could have been written.

I wish additionally to acknowledge here the cooperation of Dr. Robert A. Spivey, chairman of the Department of Religion at The Florida State University, in granting me the reduced teaching load during the summer of 1970, which made possible the publication of this book on schedule.

My wife Susan's preparation of the manuscript, her patient rereadings of the text during composition, numerous suggestions, and, most of all, her encouragement and concern for the life of this project, assured its completion. We both extend our grateful appreciation to John C. Oliver, for so generously facilitating the manuscript's final stages of preparation.

J.L.I.

The Florida State University
Tallahassee, Florida

Introduction

THOMAS J. J. ALTIZER, the "death of God" theologian, edited
in 1967 a collection of readings called *Toward a New Christianity*.[1] The title is disconcerting since the book includes
thinkers from the eighteenth and nineteenth centuries whose
religious ideas are anything but new, viz., Blake, Hegel,
Kierkegaard, Dostoevsky, Nietzsche, and Weil. The same
year, William R. Miller also published an anthology called
The New Christianity, which includes many of the same
names.[2] One wonders at first glance, what is so "new" about
all this?

It is apparent, as one reads these books, and others with the
same edifying intention, the authors mean by "new" that only
until recently have we been able to appreciate the theological
significance of these historic figures and to realize the implications of their thought for modern Christianity. Previously,
most of their maverick views on religion were set aside, particularly by church divines, as aberrations of secular, un-
churched minds. With the advent of Radical theology, there
has been a serious rereading of these early literary and philosophical makers of the modern mind. They are now seen as
"great prophetic figures who have most fully unveiled . . .
in depth the meaning of the death of God" and other radical
religious concepts currently catching hold.[3]

If this is so—and I am inclined to agree—it is strange that
both Altizer and Miller failed to include in their readings one

of the most outstanding prophetic figures of radical theology —Albert Schweitzer.

When I brought this to Altizer's attention in a letter, he replied with his usual candor, "How guilty you make me feel that I did not include Schweitzer in my anthology, particularly since he has influenced me as much as any other theologian." [4] This second-thought reaction is typical of those I have talked to who know Schweitzer; and I must confess it was my response when the idea first struck me. For years I puzzled as to how to properly approach this man, how to speak meaningfully of him as a brilliant interpreter of the modern age and the Christian faith without flattening his ideas in the press of ready-made clichés, and thereby losing his most valuable insights. Now the opportunity, I believe, has presented itself. Radical theological methods and categories afford us the means for a profounder analysis and appreciation.

Schweitzer is a radical theologian in the modern sense of the term. He has been all along. This is why he has been an anomaly to the Christian world—unclassifiably swinging somewhere in our minds between saint and heretic. Actually he is neither. He is a forerunner of many of the major motifs and trends currently so alive in theological discussions. In the past, we have stumbled about making him into everything and nothing: rationalist, Kantian idealist, vitalist, realist, pantheist, mystic, and lately, existentialist [5]—and hence we have misunderstood his uniqueness for modern thought. He is more profound and prophetic than we realized. Now, perhaps, he can be seen more clearly as a contributor of importance, and not some plaster-sainted missionary with a simple-minded, anachronistic philosophy of life. Neither philosopher nor theologian in the traditional sense, he is a thinker broad enough in interests and versatile enough in talent to "do" theology in the "new" sense of the word—nontheologically: sans church, sans Christ, sans supernaturalism, sans the Word.

Such a claim will seem bizarre to many. Schweitzer, the great father figure of modern Protestant Christianity, appears to be a most unlikely candidate as a forerunner of Radical theology. And yet, this is what I am maintaining. If this is so, why has it generally been so difficult to detect? Why has it not been perceived before?

It has, but only with a dim awareness. Many laymen, for instance, lured by religious sentiment to read more deeply in his thought, perhaps to search for further inspirational material, were like moth-to-flame devoured by the heat of his apostasy when they came too close to the center of his convictions. With singed disbelief they retreated and sullenly reconsidered.

In a different way serious scholars have long been aware of the revolutionary impact of Schweitzer's thought. One need only think of his *Quest of the Historical Jesus,* which dealt a deathblow to both liberal and orthodox Protestantism's views of Christ. By his establishing the "consistent eschatology" of Jesus, "he has aimed one of the sharpest attacks against traditional Christianity, . . . and he thus belongs with the originators of the new epoch which . . . departs from the protestant theology at the beginning of the century." [6] Apparently, however, those involved in Biblical scholarship either were unaware of his religious philosophy or failed to see the intimate connection between the two. Others who unwittingly came up against the hard core of his atypical beliefs in *The Philosophy of Civilization* signaled the significance of his insights, but they did so without fully comprehending their theological implications. They were struck more by his versatility and breadth of research than with his novelty.

There were a few exceptions: Kraus, Seaver, Buri, and Langfeldt wrote from a more aware theological perspective, but even these penetrating studies did not go far enough in relating Schweitzer's theology to the growing edge of Christianity's future forms of belief in such a way that would allow it to sing in its own new key. Henry Clark comes closest to such an awareness of Schweitzer's contemporary significance as a religious reformer with his remark:

The thesis that Albert Schweitzer is a legitimate, indeed, a brilliant interpreter of Christian faith will cause surprise, dismay or disgust in various admirers of Schweitzer. To those who regard him as "the greatest living Christian" but have no substantial knowledge of his writings, it will doubtless come as a shock to realize how unorthodox he is. To those who hail him as a great debunker of Christianity, the prophet of a new naturalistic philosophy which is destined to replace an obsolete religion, it will be a source of irritation to discover that his feet are firmly planted in the Christian tradition. The former group will think him guilty of heresy; the latter group will attempt to deny that he takes Christianity seriously.[7]

(How often this is said about the "death of God" and secular theologians today!)

On the whole, however, most regard Schweitzer as the grand old Teuton of the missionary circuit and let it go at that. They do not bother to discover in him a thinker of real importance, much less a contributor to the "new" Christianity. In an overprotective vein, some admit that as a brash, young New Testament critic he shook theological circles with some disturbing discoveries, but that was long ago and purely academic. True, he is considered by some a religious eccentric of sorts, which makes it difficult for them to conveniently label him, but such deviations from the conventional norm are confined mainly to his personal life and have little conceptual consequence. Others might concede to refer to him as some kind of "liberal," but they would not go so far as to place him in the company of the religious renegades now infiltrating the church. Such admirers, in the words of Charles R. Joy, have "forgotten that he [Schweitzer] has been the center of violent controversy in every sphere where he has moved so quietly, so sincerely, so unobtrusively."[8]

The innocuous portrait of Schweitzer which has unfortunately emerged today is due partly to sheer ignorance on one hand and overpopularization by the mass media on the other. As I wrote in a previous article:

The gradual growth of familiarity with the person and work of Albert Schweitzer has reached a strange climax: so many know him, as it were by reputation and hearsay, and yet so few take the trouble to find out what he really says and believes. Such familiarity breeds not only contempt, but suspicion among more concerned scholars that such popularization has prematurely rigidified certain misconceptions about him and trapped him between a cult of acclaimers on one hand and a crowd of critics on the other.

The search for glamour without meaning—so characteristic of our age—has seemingly enervated any sober attempt to bring his real significance into focus without exaggeration or bias. . . . It is true that those caught up in the enthusiasm of the Schweitzer saga tend to idolize the man and gloss over imperfections. . . . But it is also true that in the present attempt to stem the tide of hero worship the prejudice arising from antagonism and shallow acquaintance must be guarded against. . . . Both idolization and iconoclasm make for poor exchange, both are counterfeit coins; and in the long run such currency must be expunged from the market of fact.[9]

This is only one of the many obstacles encountered when undertaking a serious study of Schweitzer's thought. Another is his amazing diversity of thought. One wonders where to begin.

Such versatility has engendered the jack-of-all-trades-and-master-of-none attitude toward Schweitzer, which is detrimental to scholarly investigation. His range of interests is so broad and his accomplishments outstanding in so many areas that to correlate the main ideas from his numerous books on Kant, Bach, Christian origins, Jesus, Paul, Goethe, world religions, social philosophy, ethics, organ-building, tropical medicine, missionary activities, the atom bomb, and world peace in order to arrive at a synoptic view is an overwhelming task, to say the least. The ideal of comprehensiveness that challenges every scholar is made doubly difficult with Schweitzer. To be thoroughly accurate in one's interpretation of his thought, one by rights ought to have a grasp of the many fields of interest that his scholarship covers. These source streams are important; they interpenetrate and color one another. It is of some consolation to realize that one need not know all his writings in the many areas that occupied his interest off and on during his energetic career in order to understand his religious philosophy. This, one discovers, is the main path that leads through the thickets of his diversity to a common clearing at the center of his thought; and until one has made his way to this spot, he will glimpse a colorful and variegated, but incongruous and confusing, landscape.

In the third place, his religious philosophy or theology is not easy to dig out, regardless of how "elemental" it may be. His thought is at times disturbingly unsystematic and in places suffers from overgeneralization and peculiar prejudices. It is true that with patience and after many rereadings the essential elements appear more clearly. But the fact remains that there is often an aura of vagueness about his ideas that leaves one perplexed and curious. If one is not forewarned of these difficulties, many of his deepest insights will slip away and his religious philosophy will be put aside after only a cursory reading. Unfortunately, this has occurred all too frequently.

Another obstacle of a more serious nature, perhaps—particularly in viewing Schweitzer as the forerunner of the contemporary Radical movement with its activist social ethic and political awareness—is the indictment that he does not understand the need of the nonwhites in their present struggle for independence.

Like every other world figure, Schweitzer has never been free from criticism, of course. Complaints have centered around his person, his jungle hospital, attitudes, and prejudices which he seemed to embody, and his failure to be all things to all men. Most of them are petty, irrelevant, and unfounded. The most damaging criticism recently, however, has been directed toward his political shortsightedness. It is claimed he did not sympathize with the growing spirit of nationalism. He lived under the illusion that "the great white father knows best," they say, and thus he viewed the whole problem in a paternalistic manner that smacks of European colonialism.

In reply to these criticisms and in defense of Schweitzer, I would like to quote at length from a former article in which I said:

These accusations stem partially from several remarks Schweitzer made in his 1954 Nobel Address in which he spoke of the growth of a "virulent variety" of nationalism among the smaller nations of the world, and its endangering "a long history of peace."

Schweitzer has always been suspicious of nationalism as a solution to any human problem. As history has witnessed, it too easily degenerates into fanatical patriotism and becomes a cloak behind which hide racial prejudice, economic aggression, and ignoble paternalism. Such a course among the nations of Western culture has been one of the main factors of its decline. [Schweitzer, *Philosophy of Civilization*, pp. 29 ff.] At present he regards it as "the greatest obstacle to international understanding" among the leading nations. Hence his fear lest the newer states will make it their sole aim, and incur needless unrest and bloodshed for themselves and others.

Schweitzer's views on nationalism must not be taken as an argument favouring colonialism or the continued subjugation of the smaller nations. If one reads the entire speech, and his many remarks elsewhere, it is obvious he is not inferring that the colonial nations have enjoyed a utopian peace whilst under European domination, nor that they must remain silent. In fact, he states the opposite.

His solution to the problem of world peace moves on another level. He is addressing mainly the larger nations, those in control; he is challenging them to be humane enough to aid the underprivileged peoples to grow and become independent, without ignominiously forcing them to choose between disrespectful domination and fanatical nationalism, between exploitation, under the guise of "aiding them until they are ready," and abandonment. He is placing a greater obligation on their shoulders than merely to step aside and allow self-rule. In an earlier writing Schweitzer set forth a bill of rights for the African in which, after speaking of their "fundamental right" to habitation, soil, labour, justice, and education, he states that "the only way to defend and extend the other rights already enumerated is to develop a new stable social organisation." [Schweitzer, "The Relations of the White to the Coloured Races," *Contemporary Review*, Jan., 1928.] Our goal then must be the eventual formation of an orderly, productive and efficient self-rule of these peoples. But at present, particularly in certain regions of Africa, allowing them freedom by a complete withdrawal, without the proper guidance and adequate aid, would be the same, in many respects, as abandonment. The first steps in aiding any primitive people toward intelligent self-rule necessitates morally-concerned and enlightened leadership. This we have not given them, and we are suffering the consequences.

Schweitzer may be naïve in believing that nationalism is not an essential element in the emancipation of the world's long-dominated peoples, or in not recognising fully enough the danger of our "civilising mission" withholding independence too long. If this is so, then let us point it out. But it is erroneous to believe he is in favour of maintaining the colonial status of these emerging nations, in the sense in which we are accustomed to using the phrase.

Usually, to support the above accusation, Schweitzer's paternalistic treatment of the natives is mentioned: his "elder brother" attitude and his feeling that "the black man is still a child."

I admit some of his words on this point are puzzling. But I wonder if many have not made an unjustifiable leap, from his handling of the workers and patients in his own particular situation, to his views on the matter on an international scale? To equate the type of leadership which he exhibits at Lambaréné with that of advocating white supremacy is not only erroneous, but damaging to a much needed spirit which moves in the opposite direction. Having to live among mainly primitive people, still lulled to sleep by the rhythms of the primeval forest and made incorrigible at times by their child-like irresponsibility and fearful superstitions, is a little different from formulating general political programmes for the modern educated negro. His personal paternal attitude at his hospital, the result, it seems, of expediency rather than prejudice, must not be translated into a stand for racism. If Schweitzer possesses an "elder brother" attitude toward the natives, it is in the spirit "I am my brother's elder *brother*," and not "I am my brother's *keeper*," so often exhibited by the condescending air of the so-called Christian nations.

Dr. W. E. DuBois, emeritus professor of sociology, Atlanta University, though critical of Schweitzer because "he had no grasp of what modern exploitation means, of what imperial colonialism has done to the world," could conclude "that this man was (the negro's) friend and benefactor there was no question. If more of his people were like him, not only Africa but Asia, not only far-off lands but near-by slums, might be raised to decency, efficiency, and real civilisation." [W. E. DuBois, "The Black Man and Albert Schweitzer," in A. A. Roback, ed., *The Albert Schweitzer Jubilee Book*, p. 125.]

It is a specious defense of our shortcomings to condemn such a man as Schweitzer for not extricating us from the evils which we ourselves by neglect have brought about, or for not being a paragon of perfection, at a time when we could use his influence in the world to political advantage. Merely because Schweitzer has remained strangely silent on some issues of international importance, or because he apparently has no knowledge of the new generation of Africans, or of the intellectual and emotional tides sweeping the continent, I find it difficult to condemn him. To chide a man who has done so much, for not doing more, is unjust.

We must stop looking at the old-fashioned sunhelmet that Schweitzer wears—viewing it hypersensitively as symbolic of an outmoded political philosophy—and turn our attention to understanding the ideas and spirit of the man beneath it. Evidence points to the fact that his whole mission in life was a personal protest against the very evils for which his unjustified critics now accuse him. The evils of racial prejudice and European domination, which bind the peoples of the underdeveloped countries even more firmly in the chains of hate and oppression, have been the very targets of his words and deeds.[10]

The fifth obstacle is the problem of how to classify Schweitzer. Is he a philosopher or a theologian? Until recently such a question was a life or death matter, particularly to those scholars who have a pedantic passion for compartmentalization. Such critics find themselves intellectually lost without academically drawn boundaries, and they have a tendency to look with jaundiced eyes at a thinker who straddles too many disciplines. Schweitzer's ability to combine, for example, both philosophy and theology brings consternation to two groups: those who do not regard him as a "real" contributor to either because they cannot acceptably label him as being truly included in one or the other; and those who, for strong personal reasons, wish to keep philosophy and religion separate at all costs. Both suffer from mental sclerosis—a hardening of the conceptual arteries—which prevents the flow of syncretistic thought and interdisciplinary methods of cross-fertilization. For these reasons, among others, the academic Establishment remains, by and large, smugly intolerant of Schweitzer's contributions to thought, referring to them, if and when it does, with a mixture of disdain and mild curiosity.

Schweitzer could have cared less, of course, about the carping of academicians. Anyone who ignores the standard boundary lines must be prepared to bear the brunt of attacks from something in man that loves a wall. Schweitzer openly admits that it is characteristic of him not to make a "sufficiently sharp distinction between religious and philosophical thinking." [11] According to him, the two are and must remain inexorably fused in man's quest for life and truth. Philosophy without religious concern is sterile, and religion without philosophic thought is blind. Despite the obvious and often erudite distinctions that can be made between philosophy and religion, they are of importance only to the scholars, and in the long run are not essential when it comes to performing the main tasks of deep reflection as we face the perennial problems of existence. And this, obviously, is Schweitzer's ultimate concern.

If one approaches him from a philosophical point of view, Schweitzer will be accused of attenuating philosophy and misusing it eclectically for the purpose of propagating a personal religious outlook; seen from the standpoint of traditional theology, he will be accused of degrading religion in general and the uniqueness of Christianity in particular by absorbing both into a philosophical schema that founds them on a strictly rational basis. Either way he seems to lose; both are myopic accounts, and each blocks the way to a fuller engagement and enlightened dissemination of his ideas.

As I have indicated, Schweitzer is neither a philosopher nor a theologian in the narrow meaning of these terms. It is true that he was a student of philosophy and received his Ph.D. writing on Kant's philosophy of religion, which was later published. It is true that he is well versed on the history of philosophy and wrote a two-volume work in social and ethical philosophy entitled *The Philosophy of Civilization*. It is true that he has a great deal to say about ethical theory and that his main intellectual pursuit was to discover "the basic principle of the moral." Yet he is rejected by philosophers as an "outsider." This is partly due to the fact that he does not write in the recognized philosophic style nor exhibit an analytically polished manner of argumentation. This is noted by Ernst Cassirer, commenting on Schweitzer's *The Philosophy of Civilization:* "What we find here is not what we usually call a 'philosophy.' Schweitzer never speaks in a technical philosophical language. His work is not encumbered with a complicated and obscure terminology, and it does not contain any subtle and sophisticated modes of reasoning. Schweitzer's thought is a straightforward and ingenious thought. He avoids all scholasticism." [12]

More to the point, perhaps, is the fact that to philosophers his interest in doing philosophy in the grand style is passé, his Protestant and neo-Kantian orientation is suspect, his conclusions smack of mysticism, and he stands too far afield from the nuances of contemporary philosophical discussions. This bias is observed in a paper read before the Schweitzer Convocation at Aspen, Colorado, in 1966 by John R. Everett:

In all probability Albert Schweitzer could not get a job teaching philosophy in any one of the great American universities today. What passes for academic philosophy in American halls of learning is mostly confined to "elegant" analyses of logical relationships and intricate inquiries into the meaning of language. Schweitzer's concern to find a coherent world-view and push reason to its ultimate and final point would, according to many present day academic

philosophers belong in the poetry division of the literature department, if indeed it belongs in a university at all.[13]

As I hope to show later, this is perhaps less a criticism of
Schweitzer than an indictment against the main trends in modern philosophy. Considering the important role that literature
—society's first nurse—has necessarily had to assume in the life
of twentieth-century man (because of the waning relevancy
of philosophy and theology), it is a compliment. It supports
my contention that Schweitzer is prophetic in his individual
attempt to move philosophical and religious thinking closer
to the deeper channels of direct life-involvement.

If Schweitzer is neither philosophical fish nor theological
fowl, it is also understandable why the theological community exhibits the same closed-mindedness. He is embarrassingly
more of an enigma to it than to philosophy because he is
lauded as the *primus inter pares* of the Christian life. If
Schweitzer is referred to as a "theologian" at all, it is more or
less used as an honorary epithet, a sort of complimentary pass
to the inner sanctum of institutional Christianity for outstanding services rendered. This magnanimity on the church's part
lends it an air of ecumenicity.

The reasons for theology's reticence are obvious.

First, theologians in the main are leery of philosophers, and
Schweitzer to them is more of a philosopher than a theologian.
This is evidenced, for example, by his ardent defense of the
Enlightenment period and its attempts to found religion solely
within the bounds of reason. He believes "nothing but what
is born of thought and addresses itself to thought can be a
spiritual power affecting the whole of mankind."[14] This immediately alienates a majority of theologians who take any
claim to the self-sufficiency of human reason as self-destruc-
tive, if not demonic.

Secondly, theologians can point to the obvious fact that
Schweitzer possesses no Biblical, systematic, dogmatic, historical, nor confessional theology as such. It is true he remains

within the Christian perspective when he addresses himself to the basic problems of mankind, but he emphatically insists he does not "enter the lists on its behalf with the crooked and fragile thinking of Christian apologetic." [15] Fritz Buri, an eminent Schweitzer scholar, says that he is in a primary sense a "historical theologian" but modifies this judgment in the light of Schweitzer's ethical philosophy, and concludes that Schweitzer should not be judged by his theology but as a concerned critic who poses the simple, but telling question to humanity whether it can and will, in all seriousness, become Christ-like.[16] Lastly, and most pertinently they ask, How can a man be regarded as a Christian theologian who has helped demolish the imposing edifice of Christian dogma? As to those thinkers who are committed to a certain religious view of life, which includes belief in a transcendent Being, divine revelation, providence, and Final Judgment, we can fully sympathize with their strong reservations concerning Schweitzer.

In the last analysis, it seems we are obliged to call Schweitzer a "religious philosopher" and let it go at that. The term can be applied to him, and legitimately so, as I have already done. Such a general designation, however, leaves the issue as vague as ever. It strikes me as patronizingly imprecise, and does not help to make clear Schweitzer's place in the intellectual enterprise.

In view of the present shift in interest, style, and method among the "new breed" of writers now engaged in religious writing, the question seems unimportant. As Gabriel Vahanian says, "Labels can only serve to conceal the poverty of theology." [17] The older prejudices and traditional divisions between philosophy and religion are being ignored, and their survey lines are becoming more and more blurred. One has only to read the current journals of philosophy, religion, and theology to realize the surprising overlap of interests. Many philosophers are seriously applying their trade to topics that formerly preoccupied only those in religion; and theologians, influenced by existentialism, linguistic analysis, phenomenol-

ogy, and process philosophy (not to mention pop art, the
theater of the absurd, rock festivals, and peace marches), are
utilizing the perspectives and approaches of the philosopher's
domain. This claim-jumping is one of the reasons textbooks in
philosophy of religion are facing a more difficult time trying to
distinguish neatly between religion, philosophy, philosophy of
religion, theology, philosophical theology, religious philosophy,
and philosophical anthropology. I presume there are hand-
wringing difficulties in all this, but I take it as a healthy sign,
particularly for theology, which is wide open as it never has
been before. Who can deny this since the advent of Radical
theology with its dizzying pronouncements of religionless religion, Godless theology, and Christian atheism? The familiar
landmarks are being eroded, and the conventional criticisms
and parodies no longer apply.

For good or ill, the "new theology" overrides the traditional
confines that chained theology to a fixed, prescientific, inviola-
ble past. With disarming determination it is demythologizing
itself and trying to dialogue with the present and living world.
It is giving voice to many diapasons of faith and doubt that
have long resounded deep within its history. It has even moved
from a waiting open-door policy [18] to an active opening-of-
doors policy and entered directly into the contemporary fields
of poetry, politics, art, psychology, sociology, and economics,
seeking help, stimulation, and involvement. It firmly believes
that the problems we now face are too important to leave to
the specialists in religion. Whether we want to escape from
this bewildering freedom or not, whether we agree or disagree,
is beside the point—it is here. And it is the face of the new
thing called Radical theology in the latter part of the twentieth
century.

If we take theology in this new sense of the term, then we
have answered our question: Schweitzer *is* a theologian. If
Vahanian, Altizer, Hamilton, Cox, van Buren, Bloch, Rubenstein, Novak, and Norman O. Brown are theologians, then
Schweitzer certainly is. Throughout the book I shall refer to

him as a theologian, but with the stipulation that it be taken in the above meaning of the word, which in my estimation contains a broader, more legitimate sense of the religious task and definition anyway.

The last, and perhaps largest, obstacle of all—at least in coming to terms with Schweitzer as an important interpreter of the Christian faith and forerunner of radical theology—is his reticence in proclaiming his own religious beliefs. This is due to a natural modesty on the one hand and a deep concern as to how his ideas might affect others on the other. Gabriel Langfeldt, a well-known Norwegian psychiatrist, remarks that "it is typical that Schweitzer seldom provides a clear . . . formulation of his views. That, probably, is also why people's opinion of him have proved so different over . . . his attitude to Christianity. That this is so is probably due in part to a certain shyness about revealing his inmost opinions." [19] This personality trait has, on occasion, made him overcautious to a fault, and confused people by his willingness to let them believe what they want about him. Some feel he carries Paul's policy of "all things to all men" too far.

Schweitzer is unusually sensitive about causing needless anguish to others, even in the name of truth. He believes there are ways of approaching difficult matters of fact, which need not be excessively disturbing or inflammatory, and he sought for those ways. When he realized that orthodoxy was no longer tenable he always tried to speak on the positive side of its theological implications. Yet he knew too he could not compromise himself. Being passionately dedicated to truth, he realized he could not entirely avoid conflict, and this presented a real dilemma for him as a young scholar. When he was writing the *Quest* he spoke of being torn with the "painful consciousness that this new knowledge in the realm of history would mean unrest and difficulty for Christian piety." [20] "Both Johannes Weiss and I have suffered severely through the compulsion which truth laid upon us to put forward something which was bound to offend Christian faith." [21] He carried this burden with him throughout his life and even as late as 1954 he remarked: "'I have not wished to create problems for Christianity. I have suffered deeply because some of my ideas have become problems for Christianity.'" [22] The sensitivity of this suffering reflects his awareness that dissemination of his beliefs would not only disrupt an abstract "Christianity" but could demolish the spiritual support of countless human beings for whom the outmoded doctrines meant life-sustaining truth and hope.

In a rare interview with Norman Cousins, Schweitzer discussed this in relation to his career:

"As a young man, my main ambition was to be a good minister. . . . I completed my studies; then, after a while I started to teach. I became the principal of the seminary. All this while I had been studying and thinking about the life of Jesus, and the meaning of Jesus. And the more I studied and thought, the more convinced I became that Christian theology had become over-complicated. In the early centuries after Christ, the beautiful simplicities relating to Jesus became somewhat obscured by the conflicting interpretations and the incredibly involved dogma growing out of the theological debates. For example, more than a century after Christ, there was a theological dispute growing out of questions such as these:

"Is Jesus actually God or son of God?

"If he is God, why did he suffer? If he was the son of God, why was he made to suffer?

"What is meant by the spirit of Jesus?

"What is the true position of Mary in Christian theology?

"Elaborate theology dealing with such questions disturbed me, for it tended to lead away from the great and simple truths revealed in Jesus' own words and life. Jesus Christ did not proclaim himself to be God or the son of God; his mission was to awaken people to the Kingdom of God which he felt to be imminent.

"In my effort to get away from intricate Christian theology based on later interpretations, I developed some ideas of my own. These ideas were at variance with the ideas that had been taught me. Now, what was I to do? Was I to teach that which I myself had been taught but that I now did not believe? How could I, as the principal of a seminary, accept the responsibility for teaching young men that which I did not believe?

"But was I to teach that which I did believe? If I did so, would this not bring pain to those who had taught me?

"Faced with these two questions, I decided that I would do neither. I decided that I would leave the seminary. Instead of trying to get acceptance for my ideas, involving painful controversy, I decided I would make my life my argument. I would advocate the things I believed in terms of the life I lived and what I did." [23]

Though Schweitzer chose to make his life his argument and avoid "painful controversy," he could not remain silent. He continued to write prodigiously despite his active tasks as a medical missionary, and provocative and controversial ideas continued to flow from his pen until his death at ninety in 1965. His compromise did not entirely resolve the problem, but it reduced the terrible clashes he otherwise would have initiated if he had remained in the church and seminary. And he chose wisely, considering what he desired to accomplish: the ethical and life-transforming power of Jesus' life and teachings—the essence of Christianity, according to him—were driven home by his deeds. One can heatedly wrangle over a Biblical text and its exact theological interpretation, but in confrontation of a living exemplar of love and self-sacrifice, debate becomes mute and the issue of "correct belief" falls into insignificance.

Schweitzer consoled himself with the reassuring conviction which slowly grew stronger in him, that truth however disenchanting was better than falsehood however benevolent, and that in the final analysis it was something won of great significance. "We have nothing to fear of truth," he concluded. "To linger in any kind of untruth proves to be a departure from the straight way of faith." [24] Those who accept the call of Jesus' "follow thou me" accept, at the same time, the quest for truth that ultimately sets men free. "From my youth I have held the conviction that all religious truth must in the end be capable of being grasped as something which stands to reason.

I, therefore, believe that Christianity, in the contest with philosophy and with other religions, should not ask for exceptional treatment, but should be in the thick of the battle of ideas, relying solely on the power of its own inherent truth." [25] The essential nature of the spiritual life, he discovered, is "the courageous search for truth" and "open confession of the same"; the two cannot, and must not, be separated.

Yet despite such bold statements as these, one cannot fail to detect the anguish of a devout mind trying to impart fuller truths, for there still pervades his works a caution and sensitivity that minimizes the new directions of his thought. One finds in his writings a curious combination of bold commitment and hesitancy, of stubborn single-mindedness and humility, which gives the reader the happy impression of avoiding all extremes. From his scholarly manner and moderate phrases one does not get the impression that what he is saying is particularly explosive. His works on Jesus and Paul are models of theological unobtrusiveness, considering their revolutionary nature, and the threats of his open-ended theology, as detected in his *Civilization and Ethics,* are well hidden behind a facade of philosophical erudition. It is not a matter of deception or avoidance; it is just the nature of the man and his belief as to what is worthwhile saying and how it is best said. We are disarmed by his simplicity, sincerity, and warmth of understanding. His words are so fine, so readable, so unpretentiously written in such an honesty of language interwoven with familiar Biblical phraseology, illuminating facts, and personal insights that they are prepossessing, and we tend to disregard the agnostic, radical outcroppings of his religious view of life. It is difficult at times to discern from his books where Schweitzer actually stands; there are those who resent his straining out the theological camels and serving only historical and philosophical gnats.

Schweitzer, in a way, is a thinker whose misfortune it has been to be born too soon. His contributions are embedded in a nineteenth-century style of writing which disturbingly sticks

to his thought forms like burrs. Each new insight is couched in
the wrong verbal system for the modern temper. What he felt
needed ameliorating for devout ears was unfortunately tuned
down and not up, as it is today. So he continues to attract and
to fascinate people of a wholly different and much less subtle
cast of mind than his own. This is why many a one-sided image
of his thought, utilized to fit a limited horizon, has appeared,
and why Schweitzer was bound to suffer considerable neglect
and misinterpretation.

At least he never gave way to the excesses and exaggerated
claims of the angry young men who speak in the name of the
"new Christianity" today. Schweitzer's thought, like his render-
ing of Bach, is free from all artifice and virtuosity; it does not
depend upon eccentricity. He is not a professional iconoclast
nor a theological status seeker. His reactions never blurred
his vision to such an extent he failed to see his own limitations
and the effect of his ideas. A revolutionary figure—yes, but
fully conscious of the impact of his challenge. "This sense of
having upset the piety of other Christians by his scholarly research troubled him deeply and helps explain his decision not
to stand and make an issue but to go forth and demonstrate his
faith in terms of action." [26]

These, then, are some very real obstacles to an understanding of Schweitzer. They make it difficult to appreciate him as a
modern thinker of significance and as a prophet of Radical theology—that is, until one is made aware of them and takes a
long second look. And that is what I am suggesting we do.

In the following pages I do not attempt to argue exclusively
for a Schweitzerian philosophy of life or to take recent theological developments as normative. I hope to illustrate the fact
that if we are to appreciate the present trends in Christianity
and assimilate any valuable insights that may come from them,
we must be aware of the forces that have gone into the making
of our thoroughly modern Christianity. The discussion, then,
is not merely about the new ferment in theology; it is the recognition that radical and prophetic voices have been part of

the Western Christian tradition for some time, and we may now pull the security gags from their mouths and let the voices speak freely and forcibly. Schweitzer's is one of them; his time has come. The initial shock of the death of God, religionless Christianity, and Christian atheism has passed, and we are prepared to take him more seriously. Before, his insights were lost on ears cowed by religious status, stopped by dogma, and too sensitive for jarring "post-Christian" pronouncements.

Why some men and ideas come before their time, why some come after, and why some come to the end of their journey at a certain juncture is not easy to determine. Blueprints for new and renovated societies, systems of thought, and guides to individual salvation abound; some, whose time finally arrives, seem by then not new but quite familiar. Many pertinent ideas have been lying around the cultural landscape for a long time, but they do not strike any sparks and so are ignored. Now, of a sudden, many nineteenth-century radical ideas are catching hold, and we look at them with new eyes; they have become viable and fit into places made for them by shifting needs, or left vacant by traditional concepts now discredited or defunct.

In a way Schweitzer's ideas have been around for some time. Their significance has been recognized, and due credit has been given to them in some areas. Yet so many of them had no locus; their import was not fully grasped; there was no coalescence of his philosophical views with what, at the time, was held true or important. Now they have come to the surface again, this time with a strange authority and we listen to them with renewed intent; the familiar words have a new significance, and our perceptions of them rise to match his. This is due, I believe, not only to the recent changes in our culture, but more particularly to the changes in Christian thought.

I want to make it quite clear that I am not turning Schweitzer into a twentieth-century, American Radical theologian. This would be specious. Schweitzer will remain Schweitzer, and that is the way it will always be, despite the intentions of some ardent scholars who are tracers of lost comparisons. Whether his epitaph has it or not, it reads "That Individual," just as clearly as does Kierkegaard's. I use the recent developments and thought forms of the "New Theology" as a means to more fully understand many nuances of his theology that have been overlooked or underplayed. I think it is legitimate to do this. And I think it is legitimate to call him a forerunner of Radical theology, in the broad sense of the term, for reasons I set forth.[27] The similarities that obtrude are exciting; but I do not relate Schweitzer to the Radical theologians in such a way as to dispense with the differences that are as obvious as they are important.

I

Christian Revolutionary

In 1944, George Seaver, the foremost British authority on
Schweitzer, published a book entitled *Christian Revolutionary*,
in which he raised a fundamental question concerning Schweitzer, one that "presents a problem both to the religious consciousness and to the religious conscience of the modern
world." [1] "In what sense," he wrote, "can one whose critical
inquiry into the origins of Christianity has undermined the
very foundations upon which the whole edifice of the Christian dogma has apparently rested for centuries, but whose
whole life bears witness to undeniable Christian discipleship,
be said to be Christian at all?" [2]

The same question is being asked today of the Radical theologians. How can those who attack the time-honored beliefs
of the Christian church, and make a concerted plea for a
"Godless," "religionless," "secular" Christianity, be regarded
in any sense theologians, much less Christians? How can those
who can "neither proclaim the Word, celebrate the sacraments,
nor rejoice in the presence of the Holy Spirit" [3] continue to remain within the church and follow in the service of Jesus?

Previously, the occasions for such bewildering challenges to
Christian believers were relatively rare; now, with the advent
of the "New Christianity," they are becoming more frequent.
Before, agnostics, atheists, humanists, and all other so-called
nonbelievers disclaimed any connection with the church and
its tradition; now they apparently are an indistinguishable part

of the group. Before, it seemed fairly well established what a
Christian was (even if it was in a minimal and ambiguous
sense) and what heresy was (even if no one particularly
cared); now the whole situation seems in a state of confusion.
Radical voices from *within* the church are proclaiming with
persistence and conviction that the new forms of religious
awareness, which have arisen to the surface in our time, are
more truly Christian, and more of an asset than a liability to
Christianity's task in the world.

Perhaps if we can answer the question applied to Schweitzer and determine in what ways he is, or is not, Christian, we
can simultaneously provide an answer to the question about
the radical theologians. It is a pertinent problem. Indeed, it
lays bare, in a simple but challenging way, a discussion of the
whole nature and purpose of Christianity. How the church
replies may very well determine—in ways which still escape
most Christians—its future fate.

Following an analysis of revolutionary features of Schweitzer's religious philosophy, Seaver again returns to the question,
"Is Schweitzer to be regarded as Christian?" He answers,
"Such a man by repudiating the commonly accepted creed of
Christendom has placed himself outside the pale of the community of Christian believers." [4] His "ethical mysticism springs
from humanitarian sentiment rather than from supernatural
grace." [5] In essence his reply is no.

This is not an uncommon conclusion. Oskar Kraus, who
wrote one of the earliest (and in my opinion most astute)
books on Schweitzer, says, "Schweitzer's Christianity has nothing in common with naïve or orthodox belief, with him there is
no question of a belief in the divinity of Jesus in the doctrinal
sense; indeed, his whole theology is a peculiar mixture of agnosticism and animistic pantheism which he himself calls
ethical mysticism." [6]

John Middleton Murry, the English literary critic, wrote
two books on Schweitzer, both critical: one in 1948 called *The
Challenge of Schweitzer* and one in 1957 called *Love, Freedom*

and Society, which is "an analytical comparison of D. H. Lawrence and Albert Schweitzer." He pretentiously takes issue
with Schweitzer at almost every point—God, man, history, society, ethics, and freedom. He questions Schweitzer's version
of Christianity and calls him a "Gnostic" and a "mystic man-
qué." In his opinion it is most irresponsible for anyone to pub-
licize him as "the greatest soul in Christendom" when in fact
he denies the divinity of Christ, the virgin birth, the atonement, the miracles, and the inerrancy of the Scriptures. Anyone who disavows such fundamental doctrines, warns Murry,
certainly cannot be a Christian.

Of greater interest and, I believe, more revealing than his
peevish comments on Schweitzer's heterodoxy are the beliefs
which Murry finds Schweitzer holds in common with D. H.
Lawrence. They both, he writes, have "a common conviction
that we are experiencing the end of Christian civilization," and
both reject "traditional Christianity, and, in particular, the beliefs in a loving Creator-God." [7] He also notes, however—and
this puzzles many—that "both are deeply religious men" who
believe "that whatever salvation is possible depends upon
opening up new sources of love," and both "are dedicated to a
revolution of the religious consciousness—one may say, specifically, to a revolution of the Christian consciousness." [8]

To those who are familiar with the "death of God" theology
of Thomas Altizer, this has a familiar, prophetic ring, for Altizer contends that "we are now entering a period in which
Christianity must confront the most radical challenge it has
had to face since its beginning," [9] and he has issued many statements to the effect that the Christian consciousness must un-
dergo a total reorientation toward its past as well as its future.
I shall return to this point later.

Murry's accusations that Schweitzer did not make it clear
enough just where he stood in relation to "Christianity as generally understood" are most revealing. He says of Schweitzer:
"It would help to clear the intellectual atmosphere if he had
plainly declared that he had severed all connection with tra-

ditional Christianity. He says so, by implication, in his dictum 'Ethics *is* religion'; but I think he should have made it plainer than that. . . . Then it would have been clearer than it is that in propounding Reverence for Life as the new ethic he is also and equally propounding it as the new religion. . . . It would be fair to say, therefore, that Schweitzer regards himself as the pioneer or *prophet of a new Christianity.*" [10]

Gabriel Langfeldt, the noted Norwegian psychiatrist, also concurs with the opinion that Schweitzer is not a Christian. His book, *Albert Schweitzer: A Study of His Philosophy of Life,* was written purposely to dispel confusion over the controversy which raged in Norway after Schweitzer delivered his Nobel Prize speech there in 1954, as to whether he was a Christian or not. Having borne the same difficulties "over subscribing to the official Christian doctrine" as Schweitzer, Langfeldt feels a definite kinship. He takes up the main Christian dogmas, one by one, and examines Schweitzer's position on each. He finds that he does not accept the traditional Christian concepts of God, the deity of Christ, the virgin birth, the atonement, the resurrection, prayer, the sacraments, or the supremacy of faith over reason. He concludes, therefore, that "there is little point in calling Albert Schweitzer a Christian." [11] "Schweitzer has been unable philosophically to subscribe to any religion, he belongs to no confession whatever. If therefore, by Christian is meant a person who stands firmly by the Christian creed, then it is obvious that Schweitzer cannot be called a Christian." [12]

Again, agreement with this view can be found in the remarks made by such writers as James Daane, editorial associate of the widely read journal *Christianity Today.* Typical of the sentiments representative of the American Protestant evangelistic faith, he finds Schweitzer "is a man of uncommon dimension," a "deep and sensitive spirit," but is forced to conclude that Schweitzer is not a Christian and stands apart from God's salvation. Since he does not accept the Lord Jesus Christ as the

Son of God or believe that Jesus was "sacrificed for sinners and this with rational purpose," his religious philosophy is irrational and his life works to no purpose. Mr. Daane sincerely regrets that Schweitzer is so near the Kingdom, but must remain outside. "Schweitzer has sacrificed without Christ and therefore has made a pilgrimage without end." [13]

Many writers, conservative and liberal alike, conclude for one reason or another that Schweitzer is not Christian. Judging him solely by the tenets of traditional Christianity, this is obvious. It, of course, is not the only option open to us. There are other criteria for determining "true" belief, if this is one's aim. Christendom's doctrinal breadth has been capable of accommodating many variant forms of faith throughout its history, each claiming—without an excess of humility—its own superiority and closer proximity to the "original" truth. Yet these alternative interpretations usually remained within certain accepted, tacit doctrinal bounds. In the case of Schweitzer, as of the Radical theologians, the decision is made more difficult by reason of the fact that the very bounds themselves have come under attack and apparently been transgressed. Schweitzer moves beyond the minimal landmarks of what we conventionally consider to be Christian, and yet, at other times, he remains firmly planted within the Christian domain. This serves to further confound the problem.

Seaver, facing this issue, suggests in the final pages of his book an alternative. "But perhaps there is another solution," he writes:

Perhaps it is true after all that whosoever will do the will shall know of the doctrine; and that the power of the Lord is present to heal, without the adventitious aids of any doctrinal intervention, even of any historical introduction . . . to those who do His will and in whom His spirit dwells. For it is precisely because the Christian life is an unmediated personal relationship morally and spiritually, in realized fellowship with the living Christ, that those who would ask for more than this are in reality . . . asking for less. It is something to be proved upon the pulses of life, as nothing else can be; to be put to the test of experience, for it can be attained in no other way.[14]

Langfeldt also realizes that an answer to the question ultimately depends on one's definition of Christian and considers an alternative that he believes places Schweitzer *more* directly in touch with the center of the Christian spirit. If by Christian, he argues, one simply means "an ethically valuable person who tries to practice the essential of Jesus' gospel," then Schweitzer is truly a Christian.[15] And he goes on to add, "If one takes into consideration his endeavor to follow in Jesus' footsteps and what he has done in the service of mankind, and if by Christian is meant a person who is filled with the spirit of loving kindness, then he is a better Christian than most who pride themselves on being Christian." [16]

One who approaches the issue from a similar point of view, although different religious persuasion, is George N. Marshall, minister of the Church of the Larger Fellowship of the Unitarian Universalist Association. In his book, *An Understanding of Albert Schweitzer,* he does not bother to discuss whether Schweitzer is Christian or not; the matter is settled in his mind. The reason Schweitzer has been sharply criticized by some for his religious beliefs is clear—he identified himself with Unitarianism in 1961.[17] Unitarian-Universalists are long inured to their account of the Christian faith being regarded by other religious bodies as highly questionable. To Marshall, Schweitzer is a "Christian liberal," and this is the obvious reason so many are opposed to him or are confused by his religious convictions.[18]

He writes:

The main reason for the attacks on Dr. Schweitzer in our day may well be attributed to certain religious issues which have rallied persons against him. What are these religious issues that are so disquieting?

One was the fear that there was a growing tendency in his thought toward a *secularized* point of view. He moved from being primarily a preacher to being primarily a physician, and in later years he characterized himself as a scientist.

He moved out of the mission to establish an independent hospital. Many persons even today are shocked to learn that he was not really a missionary.

Then there was the fear of the growing liberalism of Dr. Schweitzer. It was in fact not growing, only becoming better known. . . .

Actually, Dr. Schweitzer was one of the few great churchmen who, during the bitter period after World War I and throughout World War II, remained a committed liberal in religion. He stood almost alone in his position, with a few notable exceptions such as Dr. Rufus Jones, Dr. Harry Emerson Fosdick and the Dean of Canterbury. Of course, the small sects of Unitarians, Universalists and Quakers continued throughout this period to cherish the values of religious liberalism; however, the great bulk of Protestant churches reverted to orthodoxy. One of the important interpreters of Dr. Schweitzer, George Seaver, wrote of an historic meeting between Schweitzer and the great neo-orthodox minister, Dr. Karl Barth, in Munster, Switzerland. Schweitzer said to Barth, "You and I started from the same problem, the disintegration of modern thought, but whereas you went back to the Reformation, I went back to the Enlightenment."

It was in this light that Eugene Exman, in his perceptive essay on Dr. Schweitzer, wrote: "In the field of theology the names of Schweitzer and Karl Barth are likely to be joined for a very different reason. The theological controversy currently engaging Protestantism finds Schweitzer at the opposite pole from his Swiss contemporary." [19]

I would like to make two comments here. First, I am sure that Schweitzer would have been flattered to be included in such a distinguished company of religious thinkers. It is true he as well as they were not emotionally nor intellectually swept away from their former theological moorings by the swelling current of postwar neo-orthodoxy. But in a way they make strange bedfellows, particularly as they all are neatly tucked together in the Unitarian-Universalist-Quaker bed of American Protestant liberalism. The label "liberal" is either too generalized and vague, in which case it tells us little, or it is used, in the above manner, in a suspiciously denominational or narrow sense, which makes it specious. Such a classification tends to rub off the sharp edges of differentiation that are all-important in such instances. Too many theologians today could be glibly coined "liberal" in the broad sense of the term; or misrepresented when referred to in some specialized sense.

If by "Christian liberal" is meant, among other things, one who restates elements of the Christian faith in terms that take account of both the original content of the Christian message and the place of man in his intellectual development in modern times, then Schweitzer as well as the Radical theologians must be termed liberals. Radical theology does reveal a lineal continuity with the older socioethically-oriented Protestant liberalism. But if we snugly fit Schweitzer into this category "liberal" and ignore the singular divergences that it overlooks, then the label becomes most misleading and tends to have a deadening effect upon our critical powers of distinction. Schweitzer, as the Radical theologians, certainly cannot be contained within the old-time Protestant liberals.

Secondly, we note from the excerpt at least one implicit similarity between Schweitzer and the Radical theologians: they stand in opposition to neo-orthodoxy—even though Schweitzer earlier passed by it, and the Radicals later passed through it. Professor Langdon Gilkey—a renowned critic and interpreter of the "death of God" group—cites as one of the reasons he believes this "new wind" of radical theology is important: "It represents an explicit and potent rejection of the dominant neo-orthodoxy 'establishment' in theology that preceded it. Thus its appearance and influence signalized the demise of neo-orthodoxy as the ruling mode of theological discoveries, a not inconsiderable feat." [20]

If one reads the many articles and books that deal specifically with Schweitzer's theology or religious philosophy, written by such competent contributors as Fritz Buri, Ernst Barthel, Julius Seelye Bixler, Hans Leisegang, Martin Werner,

G. Bromley Oxnam, Everett Skillings, and Henry Clark, one finds that all assume, whether they agree with him or not, that Schweitzer is in some real and fundamental sense a Christian, and one of its outstanding spokesmen. Perhaps they are more accustomed to wide varieties of belief and are more willing than most to make allowances for radical differences in interpretation, being as they are part of the growing intellectual edge of religious thought; or perhaps like Martin Marty and Michael Novak they have come to see that today "believer" and "unbeliever" are surprisingly alike and have more in common than either cares to admit.[21] Regardless, it is their common consensus that though he is a revolutionary religious thinker, he unquestionably is Christian.

We have apparently reached an *impasse:* some emphatically deny he can be called Christian, and for sound reasons, while others remain adamant that he must be—declaring, indeed, that he is more Christian than most.

Naturally, as has been variously noted above, the whole question depends on how one defines the term "Christian," or, more pertinently in this instance, on designating the furthest extent one can go into novel forms of thought and belief and still be accepted as Christian. But it is not only a matter of expediently shifting our definitions in order to include or exclude Schweitzer. The point is we are challenged by the very presence of this man to rethink and redefine what Christianity is, or better what it could or should be, just as we have been forced to do when faced by every seminal and significant thinker in the past. This is what is at stake, and this is the reason so many are disturbed when confronted by the question of Schweitzer's status. To state without reservation or emendation that Schweitzer is a Christian, after one fully understands his position, seems an impossible conclusion *mutatis mutandi;* yet because of the spirit of the man and the life-style which he emulated, it seems a necessary assumption. The crux of the matter is that it is very difficult, if not impossible, for us, habitually thinking as we do within the confines of limited West-

ern religious categories to understand a life that is both Christ-
like and non-Christian (or Christian and radically heretical) at
the same time. But this is what we are being forced to do, in
my opinion, by Schweitzer as well as by the contemporary
Radical theologians.

The tendency of the church to include or exclude is becoming not only more difficult but increasingly anachronistic and
unimportant. This partisan reaction on the part of Christians
is an example of misplaced emphasis; it shows a poverty of religious thought and imagination, and prevents the needed appearance of new forms of thought and response. Though I
believe the question whether Schweitzer is or is not a Christian
has heuristic value if it draws our attention anew to a serious
attempt to clarify the essential features of Christianity, in the
last analysis it is tediously peripheral. Each time I hear the
question I feel impelled to ask, Is Christianity, as we have
known it for the past several hundred years, rightly to be
considered Christian?—a question, of course, Kierkegaard and
others asked a hundred years ago. Or since Schweitzer has
been accused of being a Christian with only the utmost minimum of belief, a better counterquestion must be: Can we as
Christians grow up into such a new *maximum* of belief and
action that Schweitzer presents?

On the other hand, I must admit parenthetically that I sympathize with those who in all honesty rebel against conceiving
Schweitzer as Christian for reasons which have nothing to do
with discrediting the man or preserving the citadel of Christianity. They question the value of stretching familiar definitions beyond recognition. I tend to agree with E. L. Mascall's
complaint against recent theologians who "tend to retain the
word 'Christian' while applying it to something that nobody
would normally describe as Christianity, and then say that
this new thing is 'real Christianity,' or 'authentic Christianity,'
or 'the essence of Christianity,' or 'what Christianity really
is.'" [22] Is not the willingness to muster Schweitzer into the
ranks of Christianity at all costs, despite the obvious difficul-

ties, a devious way of avoiding the real challenge with which he confronts us? Does not permitting any and all degrees of belief, regardless of how extreme, to fall within the rubric of "Christian" do a disservice to both the new and the traditional? It may be a subtle form of hypocrisy of which we are at times unaware.

More relevant to the issue at hand is the question which so many have asked of those who call themselves "Christian atheists": How do these men differ, if at all, from the humanists? This is an obvious question and a good one. What distinguishes a Christian agnostic like Schweitzer, for example, from an agnostic humanist? When Hamilton was asked the question concerning the difference between humanism and Radical theology, he replied, "It is a humanism, if humanism means a belief that there are no viable objects of loyalty beyond man, his values, his communities, his life." [23] But he adds, "It is a Christian humanism," and this, I believe, makes the difference.

Therefore in answering the question, three things, at least, come to mind, each stemming from a different view of religion, man, and history.

First, to the humanist, Christianity is one among many forms of superstitious, cultic beliefs which at one time possessed value in aiding men collectively to face the terrifying mysteries and tragedies of life, but which now, with the rise of science, has outlived its usefulness and ought to be done away with as soon as possible. The Radical theologian, on the other hand, is still tied to the Christian tradition. He chooses to align himself, however uneasily, with its successes and failures. He finds within its communities of hope and faith continuing channels of inspiration, insight, and healing. Hamilton says that there is no difference between the atheist and the Radical theologian except "the radical can say yes to the Christian past; the atheist cannot." [24] Albeit just as knowledgeable as to its primitive origins and critical of its excesses, the Radical theologian has nonetheless more faith in its promises and future possibilities. The Radical theologian is bothered by the humanist's naïve naturalism with its superficial understanding of religion and its truncated version of human nature. He is also less certain than the humanist that the soul's invincible surmise that there is more to reality than world and flesh is wrong.

Secondly, to the humanist, Jesus is a man of outstanding moral insight and nothing more. He is viewed along with men of like stature on a strictly historical, horizontal plane. For the Radical theologian Jesus is seen in a vertical, or symbolic, dimension despite his humanity and fallibility. Because of his impact upon men and history, Jesus becomes paradigmatic of the human drama. Because he was capable, and still is, of touching and illuminating certain archetypal patterns of man-in-the-world, he is taken as the criterion by which we judge all appearances of the sacred. The distinction between Jesus and other prisms of spiritual light is not explained theologically by the Radical theologians, if at all. His uniqueness, apparently, is not due to a supernatural once-and-for-all freak event, but to the fullness of existence which makes such an appearance and human power possible in the first place; not to some special divine nature, but to some deeply rooted, amazing potentiality which is part of Life itself, made now more accessible to us through confrontation with such a personal, historical event. Hence it is not just Jesus, but the reality of such divinity actualizable in history and in us as well that is pointed to. It is not merely Jesus the man, but what we think and feel, and are gripped by in his presence and memory that lures us; it is what so many have been willing to do and become in his name that makes him the master of our spirits; it is what we are challenged to see and learn of ourselves in him that makes him the charismatic model of the human existence. He is taken to be the Lord of our lives because the power that he shows forth frees us to become lords of our lives. Such a view of Jesus is expressed by such phrases as "the first total human," "the first free man," "the man beside others," and Schweitzer's "Lord of our ethical wills."

Lastly, the Radical theologian, unlike the humanist, is dedicated to bringing about a revolution of the religious consciousness. This entails in many instances a total reorientation of Christianity, not only as to its future but as to its past as well. Such a radical revision is necessary, in his opinion, if the essential thrust of the Christian spirit is to be dynamically preserved and made part of man's future hope. This is so basic a part of the Radical theological endeavors that it is difficult to speak of in a few words. It must be grasped in an overall gestalt sense, so to speak. One must immerse oneself in their forms of thought in order to be reorientated into such expanded sensibilities. The ensuing knowledge is not explicit but tacit; it is a felt tendency toward new ways of experiencing the world; it dislocates us from routinized habits of thought and feeling.

Wittgenstein once wrote that the world of the happy man is different from that of the unhappy man. Likewise the world of the child, even though it uses the same words, is different from that of the adult; and the naïve religionist's is different from the aware radical's. One's forms of sensibility and intellectual perspective make, literally, a world of difference. In striving to reorientate the Christian consciousness to the expanding modern world, then, nothing less than a revolution in the knowledge of self, understanding of the world, media of communication, and human religious aims and the questions themselves will do. The Biblical idiom and Christian theological language, which have nourished Western thought for twenty-five hundred years and which have been based on certain assumptions about man and his role in the world, have dissolved. Hence, it is the firm conviction of the Radical theologian that further reinterpretation and rephrasing of the same outmoded world view in Biblical terms simply will no longer do. A new consciousness is required, even if it means the termination of Christianity as we have known it. Since according to Vahanian and others we are living in a post-Christian age already, the Radical theologians are bent on adjusting

"Christianity" accordingly. This is why they speak of the "New Christianity."

The statement that modern man must become Christian even if it means the end of Christianity puts a strain on the reader's understanding. It seems contradictory at most, and confusing at least. In reply at this point, let me say that it is no more nor less paradoxical than the statements of Paul Tillich where he says, "The importance of being a Christian is that we can stand the insight that it is of no importance," [25] and "The message of Christianity is not Christianity—but a new creation." [26]

Nonetheless, it is in these ways that Schweitzer and the Radical theologians are distinguished from the religious humanist and the run-of-the-mill agnostic. Also, it is in this expanded, and at the same time more fundamentally involved, sense of the term, and only in this sense, that Schweitzer can be called a Christian. Perhaps we can now answer the question, What kind of Christian is he, like Schweitzer, who has little or nothing to do with the traditionally and generally recognized tenets of Christianity? The reply is, a *radical* Christian.

A designation that sums up what a radical Christian is, if this can be done at all, is Schweitzer's own self-characterization: *"Ich bin ein Agnostiker im Nachfolge Christi"*—"I am an agnostic in the imitation of Christ." [27]

II

Theology in a New Key

I begin by saying that God is being increasingly edged out of the world, now that it has come of age.[1] . . . There is no longer any need for God as a working hypothesis, whether in morals, politics or science.[2] So our coming of age forces us to a true recognition of our situation *vis-à-vis* God. God is teaching us that we must live as men who can get along very well without him. The God who is with us is the God who forsakes us. . . . The God who makes us live in this world without using him as a working hypothesis is the God before whom we are ever standing. Before God and with him we live without God.[3]

These disturbing words of Dietrich Bonhoeffer, whose promising career as a theologian was tragically ended by the Nazis in a prison camp in 1945, struck the theological world with unexpected force. Whether it was his purpose or not, his words magnified for Christian ears, some for the first time, the ominous sound of the bell that has been tolling the death knell of traditional Christianity for decades. He was not expressing his disillusionment so much as a firm resolve to help initiate Christians into a new age which demands utter honesty and radical self-reliance. For him the world situation requires a faith fashioned on the anvils of this-worldly facts and secular duties; a faith that can speak forcibly in a "nonreligious way about religious things."

Bonhoeffer has played a unique role in contemporary religious thought. Almost inadvertently his personal pilgrimage from conservative theologian to Christian pacifist to secular conspirator greatly influenced his thinking and hence the theological directions of an era. The stages of his life have become a paradigm for countless pastors and theologians, as well as his openness to the secular world, his complete commitment to Christ as a "man beside others," and his courage under political martyrdom which gave substance to his radical statements scattered throughout his books and letters, and enhanced their appeal. Whether he was as far left theologically as some interpret him to be is a moot question and is now beside the point. The important fact is that his open way of putting things gave voice to half-submerged feelings of many anxious clergymen and religious thinkers who found in his articulate boldness a rich lodestone of new inspiration and guidance.

But he is not an anomaly, he is not unique in what he finally was led to believe and proclaim; he was preceded by a host of thinkers such as Hegel, Blake, Kierkegaard, Dostoevsky, Nietzsche, Feuerbach, Freud, Renan, and Strauss, and more recently Weil, Buber, Bultmann, and Tillich, all forerunners of what has evolved today into the New Christianity. All of them in some manner or other prophesied (and contributed to) the changing structure of Christianity and declared that Western man has entered a new age—a post-Christian age. Whether they were declaring the death of God, relativizing revelation and sacred history, desacralizing the church's symbols, de-divinizing Christ, de-supernaturalizing the world, or humanizing the Holy Spirit, all were contributing to a profound transformation of Christianity which has more and more become a reality. The whole history of negative religious thought in the West has been conjoined with the present experience of the loss of the sense of human self-transcendence, and this is what makes the criticism of the new Radicals so pertinent.

The cry for revolution and change is also the more alarming because it comes from the devout within the church; and the house of God has never been in such a vulnerable and shaken state before. Barth, early in the century, threw a stone through its opaque windows in order to awaken the sleeping congregation; next, Bultmann demythologized away the idolatrous gingerbread of myth smothering the structure beneath; and, more recently, Tillich has shaken its foundations by exposing the quasi-religious dry rot which has infected it. Bishop Robinson, in the meantime, has been leading the reading public on a guided tour among the debris, pointing out where a stronger, more adequate edifice can now be erected. Under the tolling bell in the battered belfry, the "death of God" theologians are celebrating with thanksgiving and joy the demise of God and the fuller presence of the Sacred. And outside we hear the voice of Harvey Cox and his festive bands of secularists telling us the building is condemned and calling us to a divine service in the city. In the midst of these unnerving and momentous changes, the most disconcerting thing of all is those who smugly sit among the ruins, wrapped in old patchwork theological quilts, adamantly denying that a single stone in the entire historic edifice has been touched.

Not since the Modernists challenged the Fundamentalists half a century ago has theological unrest so thoroughly infected the Christian consciousness. The ferment seethes along five main channels of controversy: the Honest to God debate, the Secular City debate, the New Morality debate, the Death of God debate, and the Future of Belief debate.

It is interesting to note that the modern trend is not toward "schools" or well worked out "systems" of theology, but toward "debates"; not so much toward massive books as toward articles and brief essays.[4] This seems indicative of a difference in temper or attitude toward religion and the role of theology as a whole—more of a searching, a tentativeness, an openness.

The first seismic shock, indicating some deep faults in Christendom's crust, was the Honest to God debate. It is broadest in its theological range and most penetrating so far in its impact upon the local churches. The founder and eminent guru of this debate is Bishop John A. T. Robinson, whose book *Honest to God*, published in 1963, sold over a million copies. He condensed and made palatable for popular consumption the radical ideas of Bultmann, Bonhoeffer, and Tillich.

Despite Barth's remark that "Robinson mixed three German brews and came up with froth," the froth was still potent enough to send laymen reeling. He urges acceptance of Bultmann's plea to demythologize the Bible, and ridicules those who see Jesus as "not a man born and bred," but "God dressed up—like Father Christmas." [5] He admonishes Christians to practice Bonhoeffer's "religionless Christianity," to apply their faith in an "entire absence of religion." "The last thing the Church exists to be is an organization for the religious," he writes. "Its charter is to be the servant of the world." [6] Thus, for example, prayer should begin not from "finding God in the gaps," when it is convenient to pray or when human powers fail, but from "taking the world . . . seriously as the locus of incarnation." [7]

It is noteworthy that Robinson concluded the preface to his book by saying although the book may sound too radical, "in retrospect, it will be seen to have erred in not being nearly radical enough." [8] Since then American theologians have been trying to rectify this error.

The second channel of Radical theology is the Secular City. Its patron saint is Harvey Cox. He urges men to become more secular since it is in the secular world he believes the work of God is unfolding, where the divine action is, and where all the important issues that determine men's lives are met and decided. The Bible, if read correctly, is seen to have prophesied its coming: Moses, Jesus, and Paul were really striving for a fully secular world. Secularization is here and inevitable. The technopolis is the self-realizing Kingdom of God. We are to greet it as a divine opportunity, not a threat, and strive for "Holy Worldliness." "The age of the secular city, the epoch whose ethos is quickly spreading into every corner of the globe, is an age of no religion at all. It no longer looks to religious rules and rituals for its morality or meanings." [9] "Increasingly the urban and secular society will liberate man, not enslave him." [10] Cox repudiates the old, phony notion of otherworldliness and the notion that the church ceaselessly struggles against the world. The Sacred and Secular are but two aspects of the same reality. Thus the reason for the subtitle of Cox's *The Secular City:* "A Celebration of Its Liberties and an Invitation to Its Discipline."

The third channel is the New Morality, or Situational Ethics, debate, whose primary and celebrated participant is Joseph Fletcher. Fletcher brings to the religious scene a reexamination of the foundations of the ethical. He emphasizes the autonomy of the individual making ethical decisions guided only by the particularities of each situation and the axiom of love. All traditional moral rules are relegated to a subordinate position or discarded. Following Kant, only the good will is absolute; ethical decisions are themselves relative. Hence Christians are no longer to be guided by sentiment or Biblical commands, but by reason and agape, or good will. The perception of what one ought to do is left to each individual; virtuous action can only be determined situationally. Adultery, stealing, and lying are not absolute wrongs. They may or may not be; it depends on the individual's motives, the situation, and the final results. More times than not, they may violate the law of love, but this does not render them absolutes.

There are five basic postulates, set down by Fletcher, which form the basis for his "new" ethic and serve as guidelines for moral decision: (1) only one thing is intrinsically good, namely love: nothing else; (2) the ultimate formal principle of Christian moral decisions is love: nothing else; (3) love and justice are the same, for justice is love distributed; (4) Christian love, or agape, is not an emotional but an attitudinal ethic, hence it is capable of willing the neighbor's good whether we like him or not; (5) only the end, i.e., love, justifies the means: nothing else.[11]

"The old morality with its classical absolutes and universals is a form of Pharisaism," writes Fletcher. "The new morality, for which situation ethics is the appropriate method, follows love (freedom to put human need before anything else). . . . Jesus taught this situationist kind of freedom from moral law."[12]

The new morality is at least in tune with the times. Its

thinking reflects the revolt against idealism, supernaturalism, authoritarianism, and legalism, and stresses empiricism, immanentism, relativism, and individualism.

Such a radical-sounding ethic from a Christian theologian only added fuel to the fires of reaction on the part of the Establishment. Many were certain that what was being advocated was sheer moral anarchy and the denigration of high Christian principles. To advocate it as morality was bad enough, but as "Christian" was ludicrous. To some it was as decorous as mixing LSD in the Eucharist, and the results would have been as acceptable.

Needless to say, the overreaction and unfounded apprehension on the part of some of the reading public and guardians of the faith resulted in branding the situation ethicists as radical and including them among the distorted pronouncements in Christian theology which many castigate as faddish and dangerous.

The fourth main channel of Radical theology is the Death of God debate. This group of theologians proclaims in variant ways that the primary datum for the religious consciousness of our time is the meaninglessness of the term, the reality, and the experience of, God. The God of traditional Christianity has died, and Christians owe their full allegiance to man. The high priests of this new religious atheism are Thomas J. J. Altizer, William Hamilton, Gabriel Vahanian, Paul van Buren, and Richard Rubenstein. I say "new" in a qualified sense, for the demise of God in our culture has been announced by Nietzsche, dialecticized by Hegel, grappled with by Dostoevsky, absorbed by Bonhoeffer, explained by Buber and Tillich, and rehashed by Bishop Robinson. Their pronouncement is only the latest in a long tradition of movements in Western thought that have arisen to correct the failures of Christian orthodoxy.

By far the most extreme and challenging of the debates, due in part to the faddish publicity it received, it is probably the most misunderstood. Altizer's now infamous statement, "God

has died in *our* time, in *our* history, in *our* experience," has
elicited the unbounded bewilderment of the laity, the ire of
churchmen, and the barbs of bishops. Whether or not anyone
fully understands the meaning of the ambiguous phrase "death
of God," or how the individual spokesmen interpret it, one has
to admit it is a most unusual and unnerving kind of theological
pronouncement. "Honest to God" is one thing; "honest there is
no God" is another.

It seems strange to insist on doing theology, making a study
of God, when there is no *theos*, no God, to study. This would
be like a sociologist who does not believe there is such a thing
as society. In our age, of course, in which a psychology is accepted that does not believe in the *psyche*, or soul, such a
trend in theology is not strange at all. There is a parallel here
somewhere.[13] Nonetheless, this peculiar challenge is what
makes the Death of God debate intriguing and fundamental.
"Despite the wishes of many theologians, both liberals and
conservatives, including the editors of *The Christian Century*,
the 'death of God' theology is not dead. Many of us may wish
that it would die and go away, but apparently it will not. It
will not go away because it is symbolic of the problems and
needs of our historical period." [14]

Each of the "death of God" participants differs from one
another; they all have their own ideas, interests, and styles,
and to read one is not to understand the point of view of the
others. This is what makes it difficult to include them together.
Yet even Hamilton, who knows as well as anyone how dispar-
ate a group of thinkers they make at times, characterizes the
group as the "hard radicals," distinguished from the "soft
radicals," which include the Secular City theologians and the
"Bultmannians and new hermeneutics people." [15] It is also of
interest to note that he includes as "hard radicals" the process
philosophers, such as Whitehead, Heidegger, Cobb, *et al.*,
who do "a new kind of natural, metaphysical, or philosophical
theology." [16]

The reason Hamilton characterizes the members of the

Death of God debate as "hard radicals" may be understood from the following sample statements: *Vahanian*—"The essentially mythological world-view of Christianity has been succeeded by a thoroughgoing scientific view of reality, in terms of which either God is no longer necessary, or he is neither necessary nor unnecessary: he is irrelevant—he is dead." [17] *Van Buren*—"Simple, literal theism is wrong and qualified literal theism is meaningless." [18] *Hamilton*—"I am denying that religion is necessary." [19] "My Protestantism has no God, has no faith in God, and affirms both the death of God and the death of all forms of theism." [20] *Rubenstein*—"It is impossible for me to accept two of the central affirmations of normative Jewish religious tradition, the vindication of God's ultimate goodness in a world-to-come and the meaningful character of God's activity within human history." [21] "The death of God . . . heightens our sad knowledge that no power, human or divine, can ultimately withstand the dissolving onslaughts of omnipotent Nothingness, the true Lord of all creation." [22] *Altizer*—" 'I really want to insist on the word "atheism." . . . Any word less than that will miss the fundamental point. I want to insist that the original, sovereign, transcendent God truly and actually died in Christ, and that his death in Christ has only slowly and progressively become manifest for what it was—the movement of God to man, the movement of Word to flesh.' " [23]

John J. Vincent sums up fairly well the overall sense and feeling of the matter with the statement:

What is meant by the death of God, at least in my view, can only be that the God of all *establishments* (intellectual, churchly, experiential, philosophical, scientific) is dead. Not simply has the "God of the gaps" gone, but also the God who is the underlying "sense" of a cosmos, the "truth" at the heart of the universe man discovers. The "omnipotent" God, the "God of providence," the "just" God has disappeared in the debates about war, suffering, purpose, and redemption. The "omnipresent" God has disappeared in the debates about science, universalism, and pantheism. The "personal" God has disappeared in the post-Freudian debates about anthropology and psychology and sociology.[24]

Is it any wonder that Altizer can say, viewing the overall trend within Christian theology, "We are now entering a period in which Christianity must confront the most radical challenge it has faced since its beginning" [25]?

The fifth storm center that comprises Radical theology is the Future of Belief debate. It is the Catholic counterpart to the Honest to God debate. Its initiator and competent apologist is Leslie Dewart, whose book, from which the debate gets its name, stirred strong reactions among his fellow Catholic theologians. "The source of shock," writes Father Ahern, "is not only the ice-cold bath of the unfamiliar but, even more, the radical changes of perspective which will strike many as doctrinal shifts blurring the very lineaments of faith." [26] Dewart did not intend to blur the lineaments of faith; he wanted to eliminate them, for it was the lineaments that were doing the blurring. His main aim is a "reconceptualization of the Christian Gospel" which demands the "dehellenization" of Christian philosophy and theology and the bringing of the doctrine of God into line with contemporary experience. This is in keeping with his forecast of "the eventual disappearance of Christianity in the form in which we have known it since primitive times." [27] According to some, his book has been a definite step in that direction.

His demands for change are extreme. Scholasticism must be abandoned once and for all. The Thomistic categories upon which the whole Catholic dogmatic structure is founded are totally unreal; they are the product of the vocabulary and thought patterns of Hellenic philosophy which reflect a hierarchical-static view of the world. What is needed is a process-historical vocabulary and world view which is more attuned to the contemporary experience of man. The key terms for theology today are no longer omnipotence, immutability, Being, eternity, or supernature, but process, actuality, history,

concreteness, consciousness, and presence. The future of belief depends upon the elimination of such ideas as the seeing
of Christianity as a revelatory message instead of a mission;
the Thomistic idea of faith's certainty; the subject-object
dichotomy; the knowledge of God and the world as fixed and
static; the absolutizing of historic events; and the naïve view
of God as an existing Person—all results of an outmoded,
Greek epistemology and metaphysics. This is the reason Dewart insists upon the "dehellenization" of Christian thought.

Dewart is doing for the Catholic traditions what Bultmann
has done for the Bible. He is trying, in a way, to demythologize
them. He is trying to preserve the essential insights of the Christian message apart from the static, historic forms of thought
in which they are couched, namely, the Greek, which the
Catholic Church officially adopted and absolutized. His aim is
to make way for a theology that can take change and novelty
seriously within its own dogmas and create the viable concepts
whereby the Christian consciousness can elaborate itself, and
produce in the process a counterpart political and social ethic
that makes room for radical change. The major facts with
which he confronts the Catholic Church are the historicity of
all thought, the openness of the future, and the creative advance of existence.

Knowledge does not unfold according to logical necessities,
"fated in advance," revealing absolute forms. Religious knowledge is continually in the making, and so is man's consciousness which continually contributes to it. This is reflected in his
views of God and self. He holds that man's consciousness produces the "self's-being," and does so in the existential experience of faith which is "an experience of God" or the openness
to the Future which reveals me to myself. "We cannot believe
in God once-for-all anymore than we can exist once-for-all.
Faith must always realize itself, and God must always remain
unrealized." [28] He leaves aside the "preoccupation with God's
existence." God does not have to exist in order to have reality,
this again is our metaphysical bias. It is the same with our

view of God as a person: the traditional, restrictive idea of personality makes atheism the only acceptable option, if such a dogma is insisted upon.

Indeed, Dewart concludes that God as person, omnipotent, eternal, and supernatural, all of these concepts including even the name "God" may someday be judged inappropriate for a theism "come of age." [29]

It is not difficult to understand why Dewart's ideas expanded into a heated debate among Catholics and why this important theological event is regarded as part of the Radical movement in Christianity.

There is one theologian, who stands in close relation to the Future of Belief debate, whom I cannot exclude from this discussion of new experiments in religious thought, and that is Michael Novak, the Catholic lay theologian. He is one of the most powerful and articulate spokesmen for the Catholic new left. His books *Belief and Unbelief* and *A Theology for Radical Politics*, for example, place him forcibly in the forefront as an interpreter of contemporary experience. Unlike his compatriots he approaches theology from an ethical and political point of view, not via the traditional metaphysical, or dogmatic, one. "I have wanted to fight out the battle, not on the terrain of Thomism, but on the terrain of the contemporary American intellectual life. I have quite deliberately left Maritain and Gilson, and even Lonergan behind." [30] "My aim," he writes, "is to come to systematic work by a long march through ethics, or more exactly, man being the only political species in the universe, through politics; I do not wish to follow the traditional course which Dewart has undertaken of putting metaphysics first." [31] This is due to his conviction that the question of belief is secondary, and that fidelity to conscience and to a creative contribution to the community are the all-important aims in the lives of men. The only authentic reality anyway, for Novak, is that of our concrete experience and our reflection upon it; the hidden God, the one "who eludes our attempt to speak adequately of him," [32] can never be found, for the question of God is the same as the *why* of existence; the search for God is a search for moral integrity, and to work for God and the Kingdom is to work for love and justice. Since belief is merely a commitment to the Christian interpretation of the world, which is not the only, or most adequate one, "action is the only appropriate vocation for the theologian today." [33]

His particular approach also stems from the claim that we have come through a revolution in our intellectual life and that the dynamics of human experience have changed dramatically. This in his estimation calls for a radical change in the purposes and methodology of theology. As he sees it, the real aim of Christianity is to close the hypocritical gap between theological speculations and religious practices by humanizing the world order, by recalling men back to the sources of their origin for healing and strength, in essence, by making them more fully human. "The purpose of the Christian life is to become all that a human being can become, to become more fully human." [34]

As to method, Novak takes the "open standpoint"—the rejection of all absolutes and the recognition of one's own relativity. The root of theology and its standpoint does not lie in any one conceptual system, pattern of images, or cultural context, it lies in a drive in human consciousness to question every idol. "A standpoint is a set of experiences, images, presuppositions, expectations, and operations (of inquiry and deciding) by which men make themselves conscious of their own identity and their relation to the world. It is obvious that a standpoint cannot be exhaustively *stated* in a set of propositions; at best, it can be shown." [35] A showing forth of a standpoint is style. Each man's is different—each has his own style, though styles may overlap. "Openness" is the saving, freeing aspect among the different styles of believer and nonbeliever alike. It is a standpoint that unites us all, for in it we "share a hidden unity of purpose": to love, to diminish suffering in the world, and to be faithful to the spirit of understanding.[36] This for Novak is the true religious impulse that must be emphasized today.

We must strive to be "humans first, Christians second."

These, in brief, are the five main debates that make up contemporary Radical theology. Each has its own impieties and interests, differences and disagreements. Each is embryonic and still awaits a more systematic and permanent grounding, which may never come. Each is a strong protest against basic aspects of Christianity. Each has had a significant impact, positive or negative, upon the church. And, however extreme its position, each regards itself as thoroughly Christian. Whatever their causes and their outcomes, the new controversies within contemporary religion are "fundamental, thoroughgoing and extreme," which make them more than neighborhood squabbles tolerantly arbitrated and easily dismissed by the mother churches.

Those who make up these thrusts toward new light are those who have wounded the church in order to heal it, who have shocked it into painful examination and pushed it, unready, into a confrontation with the revolutionary twentieth century. They strongly feel that if the Christian spirit of love, healing, and peace is to continue, as it must, it can do so only at the expense of many traditional, long-treasured Christian beliefs. Their main purpose is not to keep Christianity alive at all costs, which is too dear a price to pay, but man alive. They have come to the realization that "history has disowned the expectation that world society would be made in the image of Christendom," [37] and they are more than willing to pay the price, believing that this realization presents an opportunity instead of a threat.

I am aware that I have confined my discussion to the most recent and renowned controversies and their particular spokesmen. I realize there are many outstanding writers who cannot be identified with these debates. In the broadest sense, Radical theology would also include such diverse thinkers as Norman O. Brown, Alan Watts, Ernst Bloch, Charles Hartshorne, John B. Cobb, Jr., Herbert Braun, and Pierre Teilhard de Chardin, for I define radical theology as any thoroughgoing criticism or serious modification of the Judeo-Christian religion by concerned thinkers, nurtured in its world view or grounded still in its Biblical idioms, which stresses innovative ideas demanding fundamental changes in belief that are at odds with, and hence unacceptable to, the main bodies of organized Christianity (or Judaism, as in the case of Rubenstein).

My interest, however, is in the particular configurations of radical thought as seen in the five debates. I believe their participants are representative enough of the new directions in theology. It is true that even here the various and variant hues and colors are being sorted out by scholars, and the differences not only among the various storm centers but between the members of the same debate are being indicated, yet this ought not to eclipse the overall aura of outlook which legitimizes their being taken together as constituting a real trend in theology.

What are some of their common characteristics? Professor Langdon Gilkey of the University of Chicago Divinity School discovers that there are "five guiding theological principles" that "characterize the new theology in most of its present forms." They are:

1. The unreality of God for our age; his absence from our current experience; the irrelevance and meaninglessness of all talk about him; the emptiness and actual harmfulness of any so-called relation to him; the impossibility of understanding our experience of evil if we try to believe in him—all of these leading to the one central assertion: God is dead.

2. The acceptance of the "world" and so of secular culture as providing the sole relevant environment, spiritual as well as physical, in which modern man can live. Thus the standards that that world recognizes as normative for inquiry are accepted as valid in theology, and, presumably, the goals of the world's life are regarded as normative ethically—though there appears to be some ambiguity in this latter regard.

3. The restriction of theological statements to what I can actually believe and accept myself, i.e., the principle of radical intellectual

honesty, as opposed to accepting any statement as true on an authoritative or traditional ground (e.g., because it is "the Biblical view" or because "the Church has always maintained that . . .").

4. The centrality of the historical Jesus as he who ethically claims and guides us into the new worldly life.

5. The tendency to dispense with all mythological, suprahistorical, divine, eschatological or otherwise nonvisible and merely theological entities or categories, and the consequent confining of attention to this world and to what is directly visible, experienceable, and verifiable within it.[38]

How does the general outlook of the New Christianity compare with that of Schweitzer? How far or near are these trends to Schweitzer?

Like Schweitzer, the Radical theologians represent a shift of emphasis within Christianity which is basic. The main difference is that Schweitzer's came almost a half century ago. They have moved from a traditionally theological to an anthropological orientation; from a supernaturalism to a naturalism; from the transhistorical to the historical; from an emphasis of transcendence to one of immanence; from a closed, hierarchical universe to an open, evolving one; from a rejection of the natural world to its affirmation; from a providential view of history to a human-determined view; from a revelationist view of religious knowledge to a natural reason view; from a Biblical-centered to an experience-centered theology; from a salvation-centered to an ethical-centered religion; from the authoritarian to the humanistic-critical conscience; from responsibility to divine law to responsibility to human beings; from faithfulness to the past to faith in the future; from an otherworldly to a this-worldly mysticism.

Schweitzer as a young student felt himself a growing part of the New Reformation in Christianity. Even then he was thrusting up his solid shoots out of the nursery bed of Lutheran pietism. Renewal and innovation were taken as basic elements within Protestantism which had been more hospitable to experiment than other religious traditions. This nonconformist strain was to be exhibited over and over in his career.

After his studies in philosophy and particularly in his New Testament researches, Schweitzer as a young man knew that the implications for Christianity that forced themselves upon him in the name of truth were revolutionary, and that Christianity would never be the same again. In its traditional forms it was unacceptable. Radical reinterpretation and revision, he knew, were necessary if its inner spirit was to regain its former vigor. He also knew that the desperate, and often ingenious, battles to preserve it intact were bound to lose, and, more times than not, at the cost of the vitality of the Christian spirit itself. This made him move, often painfully so, in new directions: one toward finding a place of personal service, where he could live with his own conscience, and the other toward finding new forms of interpretation and understanding. To the extent he increasingly became outwardly alienated from the official denominational establishments, the more his heretical views acquired spiritual import. The more he shed the church's influence, the more he wrestled creatively with the ultimate, fateful issues of humanity from a growing inner strength. Eventually he set his religious task in the human experience as such, illuminated by, but not grounded in, Biblical faith or normative theological traditions. In grappling with the fate, not only of the Christian religion but of man and civilization as such, he was convinced that "a new renaissance must come, perhaps a greater one than brought us forth from the middle ages." [39] And if it comes, it will have to be based on foundations far broader ethically and far deeper intellectually than those on which Judeo-Christian tradition has rested for centuries. To search for these foundations with deep thought and illuminate them with deeds was Schweitzer's life goal. Like the Radical theologians today, he was forced by the challenge of new truths and the changing human situation to reinterpret in a new way the essential insights of Jesus, the founder of the religious tradition of which he still felt strongly and strangely a part.

III

Beyond Theism

ALTHOUGH SPINOZA is often referred to as a "God-intoxicated man," a careful reading of his philosophy discloses that for him the Absolute or *natura naturans* bears little resemblance to the usual religious meaning of the term. Pascal's realization that the God of the philosophers is not the living God of Abraham, Isaac, and Jacob is confirmed in Spinoza. Devotees have deified his ultimate metaphysical principle for religious purposes, but for most people it is indeed a strange object of worship.

Schweitzer, too, I am sure, is regarded by the majority of his critics and fans alike as a "God-intoxicated man." How could this "modern St. Francis," this "thirteenth apostle," this "world's greatest Christian" not be? Did he not use prayer in the services at his jungle hospital and say grace before meals? Was he not the pastor of St. Nicholas Church in Strasbourg and the principal of the Theological College there? Did he not go to Africa to serve the natives as a medical missionary? Is not his whole life an expression of the Divine?

An affirmative reply can be given to these questions, but I am hesitant in characterizing him by the above epithet for fear of misleading the reader. I have grave reservations about Schweitzer's unadulterated theism as I do about Spinoza's.[1] Of course, one can *say* Schweitzer believes in God and then proceed to kill the term with a thousand qualifications—but to what avail? For apparently this is what one has to do, particularly in the face of many statements to the contrary, statements that plainly war against his being an unqualified theist —least of all, Christian.

However, the inevitable question will be asked: Does Schweitzer believe in God? It is a loaded question and demands a yes or no answer which is difficult, if not impossible, for an aware person to give. All the more so since it is usually administered in the form of a loyalty oath by those who are suspicious of another's "correct" belief and want to gauge it by their own limiting categories. Attempts to point out the complexities of the problem are taken as an evasion; either one is a believer or a nonbeliever, Christian or non-Christian, theist or atheist, and that is the end of the matter. No other alternatives appear on the horizon of their limited imaginations. One of the healthy consequences of contemporary religious thought has been its aim to root out this sterile approach to the problem of God.

To answer the question with the kindest of intentions and as correctly as possible, the reply has to be, "yes and no." This will not suffice, I know; it is a loaded answer, so to speak, but it is honest.

Despite the risk of being accused of the sophist's ruse of answering a question with a question, I point to the fact that the question of God's existence leads inevitably to the question of meaning: What do you *mean* by God?

If by God is meant the Father Almighty, maker of heaven and earth (and hell), who redeems his creatures by the atonement and sacrifice of his Son Jesus Christ according to the predestined plan of salvation revealed to the prophets and ascribed to by the Christian church, then the answer is no—Schweitzer does not believe in God.

If by God is meant *a* Being, supremely conscious, all knowing, all powerful, completely self-sufficient, dependent on nothing for his nature, who determines all things with rational divine purpose, the answer is again no.

If by God is meant the Ground of Being, "the Essence of

Being, the Absolute, the Spirit of the Universe, and all similar expressions," the reply is still no, for according to Schweitzer such terms "denote nothing actual, but something conceived in abstractions which for that reason is also absolutely meaningless." [2]

If by God is meant a conceptual construct of precise definition used within a certain linguistic frame of reference for the purpose of demonstrating that the truth conditions for any statement asserting the term's existence or nature follows necessarily from the stated premises, the answer must again be no. Schweitzer gives little indication he believes that analyzing the function of a term linguistically solves the problem of the reality or unreality of God.

If by God is meant a special emotive term used by religious people in order to evoke "discernment" and "disclosure" of hidden but important features of our experience, and "commitment" to a particular set of ethical practices, then the answer is "probably so, at times," since Professor Ramsey's analysis of the term's use and function, although not exhaustive, seems quite basic. [3]

It will be noticed how the alternative definitions progressively move away from the general usage and meaning of the term. The list of qualifications could continue indefinitely, I presume, until *no* one is excluded from the theist's circle, if that is the desideratum. We remember that Paul Tillich did this, making it virtually impossible to deny God, for to deny him with seriousness is to affirm God, or the Reality that makes ultimate concern or faith possible in the first place. Without this justification by doubt Tillich said he could not have remained a theologian. [4] Many find this personal maneuver provocative but misleading, and in the end it seems to solve little. Hamilton gives an interesting twist to "this paradox which sustained Tillich" with his remark, "without *rejecting* this paradox, I could not have remained a theologian." [5]

Will it not suffice to say that to call Schweitzer a God-intoxicated man is to stretch the concept out of its ordinary or-

thodox shape, and to admit that if he *is* intoxicated he is so
by a different theological brew?

Is Schweitzer, then, a "death of God" theologian? Again we
must ask, What do you mean by "death of God"?

If by the death of God is meant the demise or extinction of
some Cosmic Reality, the answer is no. *If* by the death of God
is meant that God died at a particular place and time in history—as Altizer, and I presume Hamilton also, believes—i.e.,
God incarnated himself in Christ and literally died with Jesus
on the cross, then again the answer is no.

But *if* the concept "death" refers to the failure of the classical theological concepts which have made God lifeless, religiously irrelevant, and intellectually untenable; *if* the concept
"death" refers to the waning and eventual demise of the experience of God in the life of contemporary man and the fading
of his reality in Western culture; *if* the phrase means the revolt
against an abstract, transcendental concept of God in favor of
an immanental one whereby the Sacred is experienced as a
reality within the world; *if* it means an "increased confidence
in those nontheistic forms of explanation of man's experiences
of moral obligation, need of judgment, longing for healing or
community that the arts and the sciences provide us"; [6] *if* it
means the "death of those pagan deities that had somehow
survived in the Christian cultural conception of God"; [7] *if*
"death" means man's thinking has failed or been defective, or,
as Schubert Ogden puts it, the "demise of a 'cast of thought'"; [8]
and *if* it means being an agnostic in the fellowship of Christ—
then the answer is yes, Schweitzer is a "death of God" theologian.

Most of the Radicals are "death of God" theologians in at
least one of the latter senses of the term. Though not necessarily participants in the movement directly, all are part of the
attempt to move "beyond theism." Cox, for instance, steers
clear of the "mystical-atheistic monism of Altizer" and "the
inverse pietism of Hamilton" but takes seriously the crisis in
our doctrine of God which the idea of the death of God rep-

resents. It is for him mainly "a crisis in our religious language and symbol structure," which places him close to Vahanian's and van Buren's viewpoints.[9] "It signals," he says, "the collapse of the static orders and fixed categories by which men have understood themselves in the past."[10] "One should never weep for a dead God," he concludes. "A god who can die deserves no tears. Rather we should rejoice that, freed of another incubus, we now take up the task of fashioning a future made possible not by anything that 'is' but by 'He who comes.'"[11]

Schweitzer as a Christian radical has his own variation on the "death of God" theme. It comes in the form of an ethical mysticism, or "ethical pantheism" which he describes as "the inevitable synthesis of theism and pantheism."[12] It is born out of "elemental" reason's reflection upon the natural proclivities and spiritual incitements given within ourselves or, as he expresses it, in our "wills-to-live." No mention is made of a Supreme Being when he is accurately describing his own religious philosophy, only of a mysterious Life-Force or Universal Will-to-Live which appears as a creative-destructive force in the world around us and as a will-to-self-realization and -love within us. Everything is in the grasp of this Life-Force, this "infinite, inexplicable, forward-urging will in which all Being is grounded."[13] "Everything which exists" is "will-to-live of which we form conceptions by analogy with our own."[14]

Why does he not speak of "God" when referring to the "Universal Will"? For several reasons: first, because he arrives at knowledge of the Will-to-Live through reason and not by revelation or faith; secondly, because the Life-Force is not a thing or a *Person;* it is not a metaphysical abstraction like the "Absolute" nor a transcendence like the Wholly Other; and lastly, because the usual cloying connotations associated with the term "God" misrepresent what he is trying explicitly to say. "It has always been my practice," says Schweitzer, "not to say anything when speaking as a philosopher that goes beyond the absolutely logical exercise of thought. That is why I never speak of 'God' in philosophy but only of 'universal will-to-live,' which meets me in a twofold way: as creative will outside me, and ethical will within me." [15]

Henry Clark believes that Schweitzer offers us a "purified concept of God." [16] I don't know exactly what he means by "purified," but if he means cleansed of the recognizable features generally attributed to Him by Christianity, then he is correct. Otherwise I search in vain for a precise, clear-cut concept of God in Schweitzer. His remarks are quite indefinite and tentative.

It is true that God talk abounds in many of Schweitzer's books; he does refer to "God," "God of Love," "Will to Love," "Ethical Personality," "Ethical Will," and "Ruler of the World." But we must be clear as to why he does this. Explains Schweitzer: "If I speak the traditional language of religion, I use the word 'God' in its historical definiteness and indefiniteness, just as I speak in ethics of 'Love' in place of 'Reverence for Life.' For I am anxious to impart to others my inwardly experienced thought in all its original vividness and in its relationship to traditional religion. In so doing I make no concessions to the philosophy of nature or to religion. For in both cases the result is exactly the same: renunciation of full knowledge of the universe and adoption of my inwardly experienced will-to-live as the prime factor." [17] Hence, in order to communicate what he has to say more forcibly, Schweitzer often engages the religious person at the level where he lives, he enters into the person's own idiom in order to make his feelings and ideas better known. He resorts to the mythopoetic language of Christianity, where necessary, in order to round out his philosophical ethics, to heighten discernment, and to illuminate difficult truths.

I have observed that so many read Schweitzer from their own religious perspectives—reinforced by Schweitzer's accommodating use of familiar religious terminology—that they fail to distinguish clearly enough between those statements which reveal Schweitzer's own unvarnished beliefs and those which are perceptive insights into the religious ideas of others which he is expostulating, criticizing, or personally playing variations on for the sake of an ameliorating edification of his own ideas. Just where Jesus, Paul, Kant, and Goethe end and Schweitzer begins is not always easy at times to tell. But I believe that once Schweitzer's position is located, and this trait in him known, his use of theistic terms ought not to mislead one from his radical beliefs back into theological absolutism.

In reading the Radical theologians, especially the "death of God" theologians, I am struck by the same peculiar cul-de-sac. The less they want to discuss the God problem, the more they are forced to discuss it. God may be dead, but it takes a lot of thought and talk to bury him. There is a kind of Altizerian *coincidentia oppositorum* at work here. To get beyond theism, to the God above the God to prove to Christians that their God is dead, it becomes mandatory to speak more fully in the God idiom, to become God-conscious. If I swing to the opposite extreme, to atheism, I am forced to prove it against theism and unwittingly I emphasize the reality of that I am revolting against. Atheism is the periodic cure for the excesses of theism, and vice versa: they are dialectic opposites. This is Christianity's own peculiar dialectic catharsis.

A good example of how Schweitzer uses the term "God," or speaks of the realities and experiences which it symbolizes, is found in his open and sanguine replies to some questions put to him by Norman Cousins. They are typical of his humanistic, ethicomystical way of thinking and his attempts to bridge the gap that always exists between philosophical theory and religious sensibility.

Then, after a moment, he said that he did not want anyone to believe what he had done was the result of hearing the voice of God or anything like that. The decision he had made was a completely rational one, consistent with everything else in his own life.

Indeed, he said, some theologians had told him that they had direct word from God. He didn't argue. All he could say about that was that their ears were sharper than his.

He said, however, that he believed in the evolution of human spirituality, and that the higher this development in the individual, the greater his awareness of God. Therefore, if by the expression, "hearing the voice of God," one means a pure and lively and advanced development of spirituality, then the expression was correct. This is what is meant by the "dictates of the spirit."

By an advanced spiritual evolution, *he emphasized that he was not thinking so much in theological terms as in ethical and moral terms.* . . . True spiritual evolution means that there is an awareness by the individual of the natural goodness inside him; therefore he is *not reaching out* but actually discovering his true self when he brings the goodness to life.

This led to a discussion of man's expectations with respect to the Deity. If man conceived of the Deity as an omnipresent guarantor of the good, he was stretching the concept of the Deity to suit his own needs and therefore he was mistaken. There is no point in expecting God to prevent injustice by man. He said that after the last great war, with all its killing and injustice, with its persecution of religious minorities and the concentration camps and gas chambers and soap made from the remains of slaughtered Jews—after all this, he did not see how it was possible to hold to the concept of a God who would intervene on the side of justice.[18] . . . This, he felt, is not how God manifests himself. God manifests himself through the spiritual evolution of man and through the struggle of man to become aware of the spiritual nature of his being and then to nurture it and give it scope. . . .

To talk of the "will of God" was a presumption and often a profanation, especially when one used the term to purify ungodlike acts. Moreover, to speak of the "will of God" is to use illusion. We must accept reality. And the dominant reality, to repeat, is that God manifests himself through the *human* spirit. Insofar as the individual is able to discover and develop his spiritual awareness, he is at one with the Deity. Nothing is more wonderful or mysterious than the workings of the inner awareness by which man discovers his true spirituality.[19]

Schweitzer's disenchantment with theological conceptions of God and his passionate belief in the reality of the "evolution of human spirituality" involved him in a quest that inevitably forced his intellectual and moral concerns to move, like the

Radical theologians', "beyond theism." "It is my fate and my destiny . . . to ponder on the question of how much ethics and religion can be comprised in a *Weltanschauung* which dares to be inconclusive." [20] What does he mean by "inconclusive"?

"We cannot understand what happens in the universe. What is glorious in it is united with what is full of horror. What is full of meaning is united with what is senseless. . . . It creates while it destroys and destroys while it creates, and therefore it remains to us a riddle. And we must inevitably resign ourselves to this." [21] "We are entirely ignorant of what significance we have for earth. How much less then may we presume to try to attribute to the infinite universe a meaning which has us for its object, or which can be explained in terms of our existence!" [22] "I am pessimistic in that I experience in its full weight what we conceive to be the absence of purpose in the course of world happenings." [23]

What Schweitzer means is that it was his fate to ponder the question to what extent man can continue to be religious in the absence of God, i.e., in a universe devoid of meaning, moral purpose, or certainty. How can man maintain his creative enthusiasm, his ethical fervor, and his hope for the future and keep them from being eroded by a pessimism that is inevitable before the facts which present themselves in the name of truth to his mind: e.g., no solution to the problem of evil, no guarantee of a Supreme Being, no knowledge of any World Purpose or Ultimate Destiny? By "inconclusive," he means a religious outlook or theology that must continue to function within the impossibility of using God any longer as a religious a priori, filler of our intellectual gaps or solver of all problems; he means a world view that must remain honest and open-ended yet at the same time be optimistic, ethical, and life-affirming. This is similar to Tillich's search for a "courage to be *in spite of*," a faith powerful enough to withstand the threats of non-Being against man's "ontic," "spiritual," and "moral" self-affirmation, an affirmation that remains firm even when the belief in God disappears.[24]

To what extent does Schweitzer succeed in grounding an ethicoreligious world view beyond theism, i.e., beyond the customary theistic underpinnings and theological guarantees?

Schweitzer maintains that there are at least three necessary requisites which such a "serviceable" world view must meet: (1) it must be a "product of thought"; (2) it must be "optimistic"; and (3) it must be "ethical." From what he has just said, how does he manage to fulfill these conditions?

In order to follow Schweitzer into his particular form of radical theology, a clarification of several terms has to be made. The first is "product of thought."

Throughout the two works that comprise his *Philosophy of Civilization*, Schweitzer continually speaks of the necessity of "thought," "deep thought," "elemental thought," "spiritual thought," and "rational thought." He says he is in complete disagreement with the spirit of our age because it is filled with "disdain for thinking" and "has discovered how to divorce knowledge from thought." [25] This renunciation of "thought" is a sign of spiritual bankruptcy and is one of the main causes of the "collapse of civilization." Because of this he took upon himself the obligation of "rekindling the fires of thought," for only through "elemental thought" can man commence to reconstruct the foundations of his spiritual life.

Now, certainly no one disagrees with Schweitzer about the importance of thinking, particularly when it is "deep." In this age of banalities and barbiturates, clear thought, or any real thought at all, is at a premium. However, though the terms "thought" and "elemental thought" are charged with tremendous import for Schweitzer, their meanings are vague. It is true we feel on firmer footing when we realize that he equates "deep" or "elemental" thought with "reason" and "rational" thought. But this is of small help since these latter terms in turn are very broad. Think, for example, of the many kinds and definitions of reason there are: inductive, deductive, synthetic, analytic, synthetic a priori, pragmatic, existential, and so forth. Does Schweitzer equate *all* these with "deep" or "rational" thought? Apparently not, for there is the impression as one reads further that he distinguishes between what we might call fact-finding reason and "rational thought"—which is more inclusive.

This is not all. He brings another term into his discussion which causes considerable consternation and confusion—"rationalism." This he also uses in a special way, as witnessed by the remark: "All real progress in the world is in the last analysis produced by rationalism." [26] It is obvious that rationalism, for Schweitzer, is more than a movement in history. Though the past schools of rationalism sunk down mine shafts that produced "only metal of small value"; still they utilized *a type of reasoning* that is the "necessary phenomenon in all normal spiritual life." [27] The rationalism of the Enlightenment period is praised by Schweitzer not because it struck a rich vein of success—which it didn't—but because it "chose the right place for its digging." In spite of all its imperfections and in spite of the fact that "philosophical, historical, and scientific questions overwhelmed the earlier rationalism like an avalanche" and left it "buried in the middle of its journey," still it was "the greatest and most valuable manifestation of the spiritual life of man that the world has yet seen." [28]

This is a bold statement, certainly, even when we discover that Schweitzer in championing the eighteenth century is making a plea that we once again bring into play a kind of "elemental" reasoning which has been eclipsed by the successes of scientific or technological reason. He is emphasizing the importance of a revival of this fuller kind of reasoning. He calls it a *"new* rationalism." [29] This new rationalism "must leave itself freely open to the whole influence of the world of fact, it must explore every path offered by reflection and knowledge in its effort to reach the ultimate meaning of being and life." [30] So reason, or better, that particular *kind* of reason which rationalism employed, is synonymous with "deep thought," "elemental thought," and "spiritual thought." He nowhere explicitly defines it, but says: "It is no dry intellectualism which would suppress all the manifold movements of our inner life, but the totality of all the functions of our spirit [*Geist*] in their living action and interaction. In it our intellect and our will hold that mysterious intercourse which determines the character of our spiritual being." [31] What he is stressing is, among other things, that the inner life of feeling, the conscious and unconscious language of the psyche, must not be, *can* not be, arbitrarily alienated from the function of intellect. If the will-to-live, or our inner life, resigns itself to solitary maneuverings without intellectual guidance, its course runs aground in disaster—as we have often witnessed in theological apologetics and mysticism; but, by the same token, the intellect without constant concourse with the will-to-live loses itself in the thickets of dry intellectualism and renounces all hope of coming to a clearer understanding of life and its mysterious relation to the world—as we have seen in the empirical sciences. Indeed, the two are in reality fused together, only the modern age has learned how to separate them.

Schweitzer's contrast between "intellectual" or "unelemental" and "rational" or "elemental" thought is similar in many ways to Bergson's distinction between "intellect" and "intuition," Michael Polanyi's "explicit" and "tacit" knowing,[32] Tillich's "controlling" and "receiving" reason,[33] and Novak's "primary" and "secondary awareness." [34] It is not a new—only a neglected—emphasis: William James in the United States, Berdyaev in Russia, Ortega y Gasset in Spain, Husserl and Scheler in Germany—all protested against the narrow empiricism and abstractions of the various schools of modern philosophy which failed to explore the depths and ambiguities of concrete life and existence.[35] It is similar also to the contrast the German physicist von Weizsäcker has shown between "instrumental knowledge" ("the search for, and application of, means to a desired end") and "insight" ("that knowledge which considers the coherence of the whole").[36]

A schizophrenic split runs through our psychic and social life because, among other things, our age has lost faith in reason and thinks of it only as a problem-solving, manipulating, technological tool. It leaves the subtle nuances of thought, the vague but deep presentiments of the inner life, and intuitive insights to rot in the dungeons of subjectivity. In a false bifurcation of human reason these essential features of our spiritual life are banished to the realm of the irrational and unreal. Reason is no longer seen as a power involving our total being which unites us with any ground of reality or allows us to enter into an inner, or spiritual, relation with the world. Such a stultifying view is psychically damaging; it is slowly alienating man from his world, from his fellow companions, and from himself. Schweitzer saw the dangers of such a truncated conception of human reason—and hence of human nature—many years ago. That is why he praised the later Stoics and the Rationalists of the Enlightenment period; and this is why his ideas sound so foreign to our ears.

The second clarification has to do with the next requisite for an adequate world view: it must be "optimistic" or, which is the same thing, world- and life-affirming. What does Schweitzer mean by this?

World- and life-affirmation consist in this: that man regards existence as he experiences it in himself and as it has developed in the world as something of value *per se* and accordingly strives to let it reach perfection in himself, whilst within his own sphere of influence he endeavors to preserve and to further it.

World- and life-negation on the other hand consists in his regarding existence as he experiences it in himself and as it is developed in the world as something meaningless and sorrowful, and he resolves accordingly (a) to bring life to a standstill in himself by mortifying his will-to-live, and (b) to renounce all activity which aims at improvement of the conditions of life in the world.[37]

The two extremes representative of these views are, in a very general sense, the Western and Far Eastern cultures; the Western *Zeitgeist* representing affirmation and the Far Eastern, according to Schweitzer, world- and life-negation.

However, *both* lack a proper balance of the necessary ingredients. While the West does possess an optimistic view and a dynamic will-to-progress, it more or less takes this view for granted as something quite natural. "To us Europeans and to people of European descent everywhere the will-to-progress is something so natural and so much a matter of course that it never occurs to us to recognize that it is rooted in a worldview, and springs from an act of the spirit." [38] What is more deleterious is that it possesses this outlook without the necessary ethical counterpart and a sense of inner self-perfecting. "In modern European thought there is being enacted a tragedy, in that by a slow but irresistible process the bonds originally existing between world- and life-affirmation and the ethical are . . . being severed. The result that we are coming to is that . . . humanity is being guided by a will-to-progress that has become merely external and has lost its bearings." [39] The will-to-progress "keeps us in a sort of intoxication of activity so that we may never have time to reflect and to ask what this restless sacrifice of ourselves to ends and achievements really has to do with the meaning of the world and of our lives." [40]

Eastern culture by contrast has acquired to a high degree the sense and importance of ethical self-perfecting, but it has turned its energies mainly in one direction—inward, and has failed to reach an affirmative attitude that would allow it to release its valuable insights and ethical energy into the world for its betterment. "The deepening of one's inner life, as Indian thought interprets it, means that a man surrenders himself to the thought of 'no more will to live,' and by abstention from action and by every sort of life denial reduces his earthly existence to a condition of being which has no content beyond a waiting for the cessation of being." [41]

The ideal is for a people to possess a world view that embraces both component elements. Eastern philosophy must gain a world view that will allow the will-to-progress to flow into its fallow, world-denying fields to enliven it into cultural fruition. And the West must cease its frenetic, aimless pace before its strident will-to-progress evolves into a blind will-to-power. For only if world- and life-affirmation becomes "inward and ethical can the will-to-progress which results from it possess the requisite insight to distinguish the valuable from the less valuable, and strive after a civilization which does not consist only in achievements of knowledge and power, but before all else will make men, both individually and collectively, more spiritual and more ethical." [42]

It is interesting to note in passing how both Altizer and Schweitzer have been strongly influenced by their studies of Eastern thought. Both find a lack in Western religious thought which they believe the East could lend. For this reason, some feel that both Schweitzer and Altizer represent a more basic challenge to traditional Christianity than the secularizers, for they bring an influx of Eastern mysticism and pantheism into Christian thought. " 'From the East,' " says Altizer, " 'we may once more learn the meaning of the sacred. . . . We can encounter in the East a form of the sacred which Christianity has never known, a form which is increasingly showing itself to be relevant to our situation.' " [43]

The last clarification concerns the terms *Weltanschauung* and *Lebensanschauung*, which Schweitzer uses so frequently, and which to him are so important. Since the English language does not take readily to compound words, it is most difficult to translate them accurately. For example, *Weltanschauung*, which for Schweitzer is *the* determining factor in the rise and fall of all cultures, could be translated: "theory of the world," "world-conception," "world-philosophy, "philosophy of life," or "world-view." [44] The latter, however, conveys Schweitzer's sense of the word more accurately, since "philosophy of life" is too personal and vague, and the others more or less wrongly suggest a scientific explanation of the universe. The confusing thing about it is in the last analysis, when he finally contrasts it with *Lebensanschauung*, or life view, it is supposed to convey just that—a scientific, theoretical explanation of the world.

Its meaning changes at this point in his discussion, and it becomes more specific.

In its narrower sense, *Weltanschauung* may be defined as an attempt "to gain an understanding of the universe through knowledge or world-processes, through a philosophy of nature, through metaphysics." [45] In its total sense it is the basic, overall background outlook, concealed beneath the surface of every culture, which forms a semiconscious but profoundly persuasive and pervasive period style for the organization of experience, knowledge, and belief. *Lebenschauung*, on the other hand, is man's understanding of himself and his meaning in the world; it is the quest for and understanding of the realms of value, especially the ethical; it is the result of a particular sensitive and appreciative kind of reflection and participation in the world. "In the life-view we allow the currents of instinct and feeling to well up within us. We enter sympathetically into them and permit them to unfold their spiritual possibilities." [46]

"In what has hitherto been called world-view," writes Schweitzer, "there are two things united: view of the world and life-view. So long as it was possible to cherish the illusion that the two were harmonious and each completed the other, there was nothing to be said against this combination. Now, however, when the divergence can no longer be concealed, the wider conception of world-view . . . must be given up." [47] But, in the last analysis, it is a *Weltanschauung* toward which Schweitzer is aiming so at the end the "required" world view again includes, or more accurately is built upon, a life view. The distinction rests upon a methodological procedure to the problem: the traditional way seeks to wrest a life view from a study of the world, the second approaches from the opposite end, it is a world view gained as the result of reflection upon the life situation. It is a *Weltanschauung* in the latter sense which Schweitzer requests. One is mainly world-centered and the other man-centered; one is mainly the result of "fact-finding reason," the other of "elemental reason."

In order to arrive at this rational, optimistic, and ethical, or basically religious, world view, there are five inevitable steps which, according to Schweitzer, thought must take: (1) recognition that our knowledge of the world does not support an ethicoreligious world view; (2) realization that a life view cannot be based upon a world view; (3) realization that the basis for a world- and life-affirmation and ethics are given in the impulses (will-to-live) out of which we form our life view; (4) acceptance of the "harmless dualism" of willing and knowing, life-force and world-force, life view and world view; and (5) construction of a life view based on "elemental" thinking about the "will-to-live."

These steps, if we are to understand them aright, should not lead us to believe that Schweitzer's aim is a theological answer to the problem of God or a solution to the problem of evil or a metaphysical account of the origins of the cosmos or a scientific conception of life. He works at an entirely different eye level, as do those in the "New Theology" today. Perhaps it would help to say that in part he is attempting to formulate what Novak calls a "standpoint"—"a set of experiences, images, presuppositions, expectations, and operations by which men make themselves conscious of their own identity and their relation to the world." [48]

The first step I have already touched on. It is a plea for radical honesty and serious consideration as to how far our knowledge actually supports our idealistic beliefs and value systems, whether they be social, political, economic or religious; theistic or humanistic. Being realistic, can man honestly say that the world as he has come to know it objectively supports the hopes which have more or less accompanied him through history? Schweitzer asks us to view the facts, to record not what we hope to discover, not our own projections or wish fulfillments, but what we actually do find. He asks us to review the discoveries of the sciences, to accept each advance in empirical knowledge about man and the universe regardless of how disarming. He invites us to view the enigmatic panorama of nature, to recall the truculent and ceaseless strugglings of organisms through the millennia of evolutionary stages. We are asked to leaf through the long pages of human history and not to palliate any of the pain, wretchedness, defeats, miseries, and brutalities that we see. We must dare to look into the endless reaches of astronomical space and feel the fearful chill of its fathomless depths and the infinitesimal insignificance of our ephemeral speck of matter called earth. And if our courage lasts, let there dawn upon our puny consciousnesses the realization of the damning indifference and purposelessness of the whole holocaust. As to those naïve *bons vivants* unscathed as yet by the world's slow stain, who live in unfounded optimism, Schweitzer bids them to "direct their gaze to the barred windows of insane asylums," to walk the miles and miles of hospital corridors lined with the sick and the dying, and to remember all the other ceaseless horrors to which flesh is heir.

Unrest, disappointment and pain are our lot in the short span of time which lies between our entrance on life and our departure from it. What is spiritual is in a dreadful state of dependence on our bodily nature. Our existence is at the mercy of meaningless happenings and can be brought to an end by them at any moment. The will-to-live gives me an impulse to action, but the action is just as if I wanted to plow the sea, and sow in the furrows. What did those who worked before me effect? What significance in the endless chain of world happenings have their efforts had? With all its illusive promises, the will-to-live only means to mislead me into prolonging my existence and allowing to enter on existence other beings to whom the same miserable lot has been assigned . . . so that the game may go on and on.[49]

Here are the facts which Schweitzer asks us to face. Taking them into account, can we find any purpose in the world process? Can we discover within it any meaning it may have for our lives? Do we find any explanation or solution for the problems of evil? Is it possible to establish upon the knowledge we gather a stable world view which is optimistic and ethical? His answer is, "No."

This is not the first time that the problem of evil has rumbled like a boulder onto the path of belief and forced its travelers to abandon the Way of Him who promises to make all paths plain. The most ardent Christian apologist is silenced in mid-faith by the death cry of one innocent child, even as Alyosha in *Brothers Karamazov*. It is the senseless and inexplicable suffering of humans and the wanton destructiveness of nature that stops Schweitzer, Hamilton, Rubenstein, and Novak in their theistic tracks and makes them wince agnostically. For Novak, "the fact of evil is an apparent defeat for understanding and hence for God. Why does he tolerate such defeats?" he asks; "we cry out in desperation: 'Say something clearly. Speak!' There never is an answer." [50] "The insurmountable barrier to Christianity does seem to me to be the problem of evil," writes Hamilton quoting Camus. The enigma is painful and defeating enough without the belief in an omnipotent and benevolent God, but with him, it is intolerable. Either he is hopelessly indifferent or sadistically cruel.

Both Hamilton and Novak, with great sensitivity and painful honesty, review again the classical theistic answers and show step by step their inadequacy, which they are forced, in the name of all that is sane and just, to abandon. They prefer to live in the *absence* of that kind of Deity; they seek for other forms of explanation which will at least not insult one's intelligence, nor inadvertently turn God into the devil. The alternatives are not particularly easy or satisfying. Says Hamilton: "The special power of the problem of suffering is that it can really dry up in a man any capacity or wish to call out for the presence of God. If theology cannot reshape its statements about God to face this fact, many men will continue to prefer some sort of humanism without answers to a correct doctrine of God without answers." [51] And Novak writes: "Our problem is whether to disbelieve in God because of the fact of evil, or to believe in him in spite of it. The irony is that in either case one must, if one is to justify one's life, remain faithful to understanding, friendship, and creativity. One must be resigned to those tragedies one cannot prevent." [52] For Rubenstein the problem of evil and suffering played an especially significant role in his theological development. The events that took place in the first half of the twentieth century, particularly in Hitler's death camps, were the final blows to the credibility of belief in a benevolent God for him. "The human evil perpetrated in those years could not be dismissed as a sport of history. Man's image of himself and of God was permanently impaired by what took place." [53]

I am struck by the similar attitudes and responses these men share with Schweitzer; not only in their sensitivity toward human suffering and the insolvable problem of nonmoral evil, but there is the same feeling of frustration and futility with the traditional theological answers, the same demand for completer honesty and intellectual integrity, and the drawing of the same raw conclusions with rare courage.

Invariably, then, there follows the second step which is the realization that "neither world- and life-affirmation nor ethics can be founded on what our knowledge of the world can tell us." [54] Schweitzer openly admits that he cannot "get beyond this renunciation of knowledge of the universe." [55] He resigned himself to the fact that there is no way to gain from an analysis of the universe and on the basis of the natural sciences a knowledge of a perfect creative First Cause of the universe, moral law, and a world plan with unending human progress as its ultimate purpose. Whatever life view man works out, it will have to leave this hope aside; it will have to remain forever inconclusive. We must make up our minds that an understanding of life's meaning cannot come from our knowledge of the physical world which fails to support, and at times even opposes, our creaturely aspirations and moral incentives. For centuries Western thinkers have lived on in an intoxication of belief that both the outer world and the inner world could be scientifically unified into one complete, logically consistent system. This Schweitzer knew was an illusion, an impossibility. He wrote in a letter to me, "That progress in the scientific knowledge of the world could only bring us more deeply an awareness of its fundamental mystery, I realized already in 1900 before one had any idea about the discoveries of Planck and Einstein." [56]

Efforts to unite the two resulted either in an optimistic but mythological interpretation of the world; a subtle but specious monism that either mentalized matter or materialized mind; the postulation of a metaphysical *deus ex machina* that somehow united the two; or in a skepticism that prided itself on its "realism" but left man to stumble hopelessly about in the dark. "Thought of former times aimed at intellectual comprehension of the world. . . . But these hopes are doomed to failure. We are not destined to attain to such an understanding of the objective world and ourselves as forming a mutual harmony." [57]

For Schweitzer the vestibule through which thought must travel into the cynosure of world- and life-affirmation and ethics is resignation. We must resign ourselves "to live before God without God," to live religiously without religion, to live, even though there is no immortality, like men who deserved it, to live as men morally called to great deeds in the absence of a divine Lawgiver or heavenly rewards—or as Schweitzer puts it: we must resign ourselves to the fact that our life view cannot be united with our world view. "Necessity bids us cut the tow rope and try to let life-view continue its voyage independently." [58]

"Although Schweitzer looked back to the eighteenth century with nostalgia," writes Professor John Everett, "he was an intensely modern agnostic."

Sophisticated contemporary minds are just as skeptical and just as wary of knowledge as Schweitzer. They know that it is not now possible to fit all facts together into a neat non-contradictory interrelated whole that automatically speaks its own meaning. They know the tricky and self-deluding nature of such words as "law," "cause" and "explanation." Modern historians would agree with Schweitzer that no matter how well documented an historic event

may be we can only have the barest glimpse of what actually happened. Modern scientists would agree that they too find no purpose or ultimate meaning in the booming, buzzing, destructive and
creative spectacle of forces which we call a world. And very few
social scientists would argue with his conclusions that knowledge
of the shifts and turns in the affairs of men does not lead to an
understanding of the meaning and purpose of life.[59]

So our thinking turns away, in the third step, from what the
outer events in the world alone tell us to a contemplation of
what our inner natures reveal. If the world will not furnish
us with the required knowledge, there is that aspect of nature
which perhaps will—man. Schweitzer moves to reinstate man
once again at the center of the universe from which he has
been estranged. We have been so eager in our searchings for
clues in the world of science, history, and society that we have
forgotten that mysterious agent who is doing the searching;
so lost in the theological clouds seeking divine assurances that
we have overlooked the phenomenon that is the sole interpreter and final arbiter of all divine-human encounters; or,
ensconced in metaphysical and ideological systems looking for
transcendental answers, that we have forgotten who the system builder is. If we desire a secure foundation for our ethical
principles, do we not find it potentially in the nature of man?
If affirmation of our existence and of the world is so necessary,
is it not found already sleeping in our wills-to-live? If we search
for purpose and meaning, is it not discovered in that mysterious
part of the makeup of the universe called man? Our life view
need not be founded exclusively "out of items of knowledge
gathered from the world," but can rest securely upon the facts
that are gained from an analysis of the nature and function
of the will-to-live within us. "There are given in it values and
incitements bearing on my relation to the world and to life
which find no justification in my reflection upon the world and
existence." [60]

In this way, our life view is not deductively dependent on
an objective view of the world in a logically unified sense;

we no longer uselessly waste time trying to harmonize the dissonances between world process and what we know and will out of the mysterious stirrings of life-forces within us. An "optimistic-ethical world-view" need not be a product of frantic willing or leaps of faith. The life-force which swells within me and in all life cries for recognition. Schweitzer bids us take the logico-empirico-metaphysico-supertechnological gag of choking objectivity from its mouth and let it speak: it affirms life, it wills to live, it contains stirrings of ethical impulses in its will-to-perfection, it has the potentialities for creative activity, deepened sensitivities. Within man these elements often appear to be absent, for they are sleeping; but they can be awakened into full activity by consciousness which learns to think deeply enough about itself and its relation to the world.

Pessimism, according to Schweitzer, is now inconsistent. Why is this? There is given in our natures what Schweitzer calls "*simple* world- and life-affirmation." This is not a matter of choice; it is forced upon us, we are alive, we exist, every heartbeat is an affirmation of life. The peculiar urge within us, and all about us, throbs to live, to expend its energy, to seek further existence, to realize itself. If we were consistent with our pessimism which finds life meaningless and absurd, we would commit suicide. But "the will-to-live is stronger than the pessimistic facts of knowledge. An instinctive reverence for life is within us, for we are will-to-live." [61]

This does not say that pessimism vanishes just because we have found it to be inconsistent, for "pessimistic knowledge pursues us closely right on to our last breath." [62] Nor does the fact that we are urges to live banish despair and lead us to a deepened affirmation. "We begin our life-course in an unsophisticated world- and life-affirmation. The will-to-live which is in us gives us that as natural. But later, when thought awakens, questions crop up which make a problem of what has hitherto been a matter of course. What meaning will you give your life? What do you mean to do in the world? When, along with these questions, we begin trying to reconcile knowledge and will-to-live, facts get in the way with confusing suggestions." [63] And, "whenever the *deepened* world- and life-affirmation is not reached, that remains only a depreciated will-to-live, which is not equal to the tasks of life." [64] But if we wish to be consistent with the primary affirmation, which is in the very cells of our being, we will also affirm life and strive to lift it to its highest level. "If man affirms his will-to-live, he acts naturally and honestly. He confirms an act which has already been accomplished in his *instinctive* thought by repeating it in his *conscious* thought." [65] This source of world- and life-affirmation and of ethics, however, to be of any value must be brought to full consciousness and developed. "There are two things which thought has to do for us; it must lead us from the naïve to a deepened world- and life-affirmation; and must let us go on from mere ethical impulses to an ethic which is a necessity of thought." [66]

The fourth step, which is the demand that we recognize the dualism of "willing and knowing," life view and world knowledge, is most misleading if one is not forewarned of an apparent contradiction in Schweitzer's thought and his tendency to overstate his case. If we accept him at face value without emendation, his dualism does not remain as "harmless" as he believes. The danger of so doing is typified in many of his critics, such as John Middleton Murry and Oskar Kraus, to name two, who find that Schweitzer's whole ethical philosophy is nothing but the result of sheer emotional feeling and irrational willing. Disillusioned by the failures of theology, philosophy, and science, Schweitzer, they say, guarantees that life and existence have value in themselves by a strange "mysticism of the will." [67] Such an interpretation is understandable considering many of Schweitzer's remarks and the exaggerated division he creates between world view and life view. But it is wrong; due, I am sure, to a misunderstanding of what he means by "ethical mysticism," "elemental reason," and "will-to-live." This in turn leads to a misunderstanding of his so-called "dualism," which I want to avoid, if possible.

Kraus, for example, believes that "in the true mystic manner" Schweitzer's religious philosophy "abandons the sound basis of strict scientific knowledge and accepts sources of cognition which lay no claim to logical value . . . whether it is a question of ecstasies, of visions, intuition, of seeing with the mind or a 'mysterious experience,' the question of logical justification remains the same." [68] So he concludes, "We have no other choice in Schweitzer's case but to speak of a 'groundless optimism.'" [69]

There are two things amiss here. First, to regard Schweitzer as a "mystic" in the usual religious sense of the term is to do him a gross disservice. His mysticism is an "ethical mysticism" or a "mysticism of reality," which is something quite different. The emphasis is on *ethical* and *reality*, not mystical. It is a capsulized expression of his ethic of Reverence for Life which seeks through concrete ethical action to become united with all forms of life which are regarded, under the aegis of the Universal Will-to-Live, as One. It is more a spiritual attitude, an outlook, a world view expressed by the phrase "all Life is One," as when regarded in a biological sense. Perhaps this is the meaning of Schweitzer's strange remark when, pointing to the picture of Darwin which he kept above his bed, he said, "He saw the truth." It has nothing to do with visions, ecstasies, flights of the soul, satori, "seeing with the mind," nor does it involve any of the esoteric, gnostic, theosophical, or *via negativa* kinds of knowledge or ways of knowing. Such forms of mystical activity are subjective and otiose; they lead away from actual life, not toward it. This is "traditional" or "abstract mysticism." "Experience of becoming one with the Absolute, of existence within the world-spirit, or absorption into God, or whatever one may choose to call the process," [70] ". . . becomes a pure act of consciousness, and leads to a spirituality which is just as bare of content as the hypothetical Absolute." [71] Schweitzer seeks an inward relationship to the world, but not through imaginative, symbolic, superintellectual, abstract ways. Only through giving of ourselves as men to other men, only through concrete ethical acts can we achieve a living and real relationship. "Mysticism is not a friend of ethics but a foe," writes Schweitzer. "It devours ethics." [72] This is the reason he believes, "We must therefore abandon abstract mysticism, and turn to the mysticism which is alive." [73]

In his Hibbert Lectures, which Schweitzer delivered at Oxford University in 1934, he discussed "four 'paths' along which thinking seeks to arrive at religion," all of them unsuccessful: materialism—"the religion of natural science"; Kantianism—which "lacks compulsive power and enthusiasm" and "cannot be placed in the center of things"; pragmatism—which "asserts that there are spiritual truths alongside theoretical truths, and that all valuable conviction has truth in itself—a dangerous assertion"; and mysticism. Here is what he has to say about the last:

The fourth path is that trodden by modern thinkers emancipated from Kant. They are obscure thinkers—their thinking is obscure and, moreover, they have a talent of writing obscurely! They want to get at religion by saying: All this knowledge of the world through science is only a description of the world, from which man derives nothing. What we must know is the essential nature of the universe. The thing we must be occupied with is the mystery of our life. How we understand the mystery of our life is the mystery of the universe. They say: We know the universe by intuition, not by reason. Our life knows the life in the world, and through our life we become one with the life of the universe. This thinking therefore is mysticism.

But ethics plays no part in this form of thought. The great problem of what man is aiming at plays no part in it.[74]

When Schweitzer speaks of ethics—in its fullest sense—it is synonymous with religion. Reverence for Life is for him not just an ethic, it is a religion. "The view of Reverence for Life is ethical mysticism. It allows union with the infinite to be realized by ethical action. This ethical mysticism originates in logical thinking." [75]

Secondly, it is strange that Kraus places the "scientific process of thought" at one end in contradistinction to the mystical or "non-scientific" process at the other. The implication is that if one does not approach every problem in the strict scientific manner, he is *ipso facto* an irrational mystic. There are certainly other approaches, or combinations of approaches. Kraus has disregarded Schweitzer's discussion of the word "rational" or defined it in too narrow a sense. I already have mentioned Schweitzer's broader interpretation in hope that this error could be avoided. Plainly, Schweitzer's "rational basis for optimistic thought" *does* lay "claim to a scientific process of thought," for, as he wrote, rational thought must leave itself freely open "to the whole influence of the world of fact"; [76] it must take into account the existential fact of the will-to-live, to determine if we can arrive in this manner at a religious interpretation of life. Schweitzer does not propose a world view based exclusively upon what science tells us—first, because this is not its aim or function and second, because he knows it is futile. What I am maintaining is that in Schweitzer's "rational" approach to the problem he does not exclude the normal, scientific, fact-finding processes of the mind, nor the knowledge gained in this manner.[77] Even if, for Schweitzer, "practical reason" takes precedence in face of the present task over "theoretical reason," he is not a mystic, nor a rationalist in the sense in which it is often unduly connected with the belief that the mind possesses inherent powers capable of formulating universal principles apart from actual experience.

These criticisms of Kraus, however, do not dispel the difficulties that surround Schweitzer's dualism of "knowing and willing" which remains for him an irreconcilable fact of experience. I admit that unless a clearer connotation is given to what he means by "world-knowledge" or "the facts," the dichotomy existing between world view and life view is epistemologically disastrous. We may with Schweitzer renounce any attempt to understand the world totally, or to "write out a birth certificate for the universe"; we may agree that if we remain honest, nature does not show itself amenable to a smooth solution concomitant with an optimistic-ethical interpretation, but this does not give us license to sever ourselves completely from the world or to proceed to interpret it in any manner our desires see fit.

If Schweitzer means what his words say, that we must "cut the tow rope" between life view and world view, and allow life view to continue its voyage independently, this leads to a blind subjectivism or an untenable solipsism. No view of life, religious philosophy, or value system can wall itself off from the world and spin out an adequate *Weltanschauung. All* opinions, impressions, intuitions, ideas, and beliefs, in order to merit the title of knowledge, whether gained from observation of the world or from incitements and impressions of the psyche, must meet the tests pertaining thereto, such as consistency, coherence, congruence, and assimilability and agreement with other knowledge facts.

If, however, Schweitzer means by this phrase, as I believe he does, that in the formulation of our philosophy of life we must not on the one hand inordinately allow the dysteleological forces of the world to encroach upon and destroy the natural affirmation of life within us, nor overcome our natural incentives of self-development and moral activity, nor disperse the natural purposiveness which we can and do give our lives; and if he means on the other hand that we must not be misled by the exaggerated and insular claims of the operational symbol systems of scientific objectivity and the fantastic metaphysical schools of natural philosophy which follow in its wake, into believing that "someday" a complete total view will be fashioned in which the inner will become the outer, and fact and value will be joined in holy wedlock and live in eternal bliss—if he means only these things, *then* he escapes the criticisms of his unjustified detractors.

To substantiate this, I am forced to cite a gross inconsistency in Schweitzer's thought (a strange procedure, indeed!). He says: "In the world we can discover *nothing* of any purposive evolution in which our activities can acquire a meaning. Nor is the ethical to be discovered in *any* form of the world-process," [78] and then he turns around and proceeds to build not only an ethic, but a world view, upon the "will-to-live" which is an ethical urge in man. He even goes so far, as we have seen, as to claim that this ethical and world-affirming life-force is in everything.

Even if we interpret him to mean that though the will-to-live is found in everything, it is only as it is found in man that it becomes meaningful, or that man must work out his own pattern of life since there is no cosmic blueprint except his own creativeness, we still must agree with John Middleton Murry's criticism of Schweitzer, "that nature philosophy cannot be made to yield a real ethic . . . is only true on one important condition: that man himself is excluded from nature." [79] Because of his peculiar and at times extreme division between world view and life view, this is what he has done—and it has led him into an inconsistency. One can legitimately, for theoretical purposes, separate practical and theoretical reason, science and value philosophy, inner and outer experience, but one cannot view man as separate from the "world-process." (Schweitzer does not realize how heavily he leans upon nature philosophy in the construction of his own radical theology.) He *does* discover the ethical within the "world-process," for he bases his ethic upon the will-to-live, found not only in man but in its other forms throughout the universe as well.

There are advantages in bringing to mind the importance of keeping value judgments and judgments of fact in distinction, I presume. We also agree with him that an overall philosophy of life and a universal system of ethics must need spring from some knowledge more comprehensive in scope than that which the descriptive sciences bring. But to emphasize *de jure* judgments in exclusion of *de facto* judgments is not sound. The meaning of life and not factual knowledge of the cosmos may take precedence in the exigencies of daily living, but the two cannot be so compartmentalized. Nor are the methods involved in such undertakings totally different from each other. The division which Schweitzer makes between them all is not categorical, as we have seen by his own felicitous inconsistency, but it is, to be sure, extreme.

What can we conclude, then, about this so-called dualism?

First, it is attitudinal and not epistemological or cosmological; it is the eventual casting of one's lot with the facts that support a religious world view over against the facts that lead to pessimism. This exaggerated bifurcation which he creates, he believes protects and guarantees the needed optimism and ethical enthusiasm for an active and adequate philosophy of life.

Secondly, it is not a dualism of "willing and knowing" as he himself labels it and, understandably, as Kraus and others have been misled to believe; it is one of "knowing and knowing"—what we "know" objectively about the world and what we "know" existentially about human life. As I have said, the two ways of knowing are not so estranged or different that we can accuse Schweitzer of resorting in the last analysis to irrationalism or mysticism—it is only Schweitzer's way of writing which unfortunately makes them appear that way. One wishes he had avoided the whole issue and found some other way to express his frustrations against the limitations of science and natural philosophy. He could have saved his readers a great deal of trouble and himself from falling into an inconsistency.

Thirdly, it is very misleading, for not only is this dualism *not* epistemological or cosmological, but his whole ethical philosophy strongly reflects a *monistic* attitude, particularly when it assumes the form of an ethical pantheism, as we shall see in an analysis of "will-to-live" and discussion of his ethic of Reverence for Life.

Before discussing Schweitzer's fifth step, which leads to the heart of his radical theology, I want to mention several similarities between his method of approach to the problem of God and that of the Radical theologians.

The first pertains to their orientation. If one word characterizes it, it might be anthropological, as contrasted with theological. Even Schweitzer, who expects everything from rational thought and philosophy, employs a type of man-centered orientation which is very close to what is known today as philosophical anthropology. Another term might be humanistic, since all of them believe that the major focus of theology is not God but man, and that the soundest clues to any divine principle are found in man and the world, and nowhere else. This is certainly in part due to the influence of existentialism as expressed in the philosophy of Heidegger, Sartre, Jaspers, and Marcel, and in the theology of Tillich, called the father of Radical theology, who unmasked God to reveal humanity.

The humanism at work in Schweitzer and in Radical theology, however, unfolds under the aegis of the Christian world view, and an ethical quest for its Christological problems, and this is what makes it unique and stubborn to classify. It is a humanism living within the dynamics of a revised eschatological impetus, among other things. Schweitzer could write to the American Humanist Association that the world is deceived if it believes it can "raise itself above Humanism," for "only ethics and religion which include in themselves the humanitarian ideal have true value," [80] but Schweitzer's own religious ethics moves under the protectorate of the world view of ethical mysticism which ontologically grounds it in reality. Tillich's words underscore Schweitzer's own thinking where he writes: "Man has become aware of the fact that he himself is the door to the deeper levels of reality, that in his own existence he has the only possible approach to existence itself. . . . The immediate experience of one's own existing reveals something of the nature of existence generally." [81]

Nonetheless the *modus vivendi* of Radical theology's approach to the problem of God has a new air about it, a new epicenter. It is almost as if they turn their backs on God in order to discover him more fully in the world; deny him in order to affirm in new ways; bury him in order to resurrect man in his

image; or intentionally ignore the whole theistic debate in or-
der to vivify for modern man the need to become religious.
At least they declare a positive belief in the irrelevance of the
God issue; it is no longer a viable option. As Cox expresses it:
"My own response to the dead-end signaled by the 'death of
God' mood is to continue to move away from any spatial sym-
bolization of God and from all forms of metaphysical dualism.
I am trying to edge cautiously toward a secular theology, a
mode of thinking whose horizon is human history and whose
idiom is 'political' in the widest Aristotelian sense of that term,
i.e., the context in which man becomes fully man." [82]

The question is no longer, as Tillich forcibly propounds,
whether God exists or does not exist, or whether man can make
any true or false statements about him, or even what is *meant*
by the term "God"—since all God talk is held in suspicion. It is
the *meaning* of the question-asker man, and the meaning of
the questions themselves, and the meaning of the whole phenomenon of man's search for love, power, and justice that is
more important and revelatory. Man's quest for knowledge and
wisdom, for healing and sanity, for creativeness and moral
self-realization *is* the quest for God. There is no separate quest,
or path, apart from these as theologians have traditionally
maintained. The Radicals refuse to sacrifice, as did Barth, man's
freedom for God's sovereignty, the natural world for a realm
of grace. The transcendent God of theological belief, the
Wholly Other, is wholly other than the interests of the New
Theology. This God is no longer beyond man, man is beyond
God, beyond theism. And as Schweitzer and others have
pointed out, men are left unfortunately to cope with the problems and dilemmas that such a false venture has left in its
wake. "God is man's failure," as Vahanian has said, and we
are the victims of our own religious and cultural illusions.

One can say that for the Radical theologians, as well as for
Schweitzer, the problem of God is the same as the problem of
man or the *why* of human existence. [83]

The second similarity between them is their strong prejudice against metaphysics. There are very few exceptions to this among the Radical theologians. They would agree with Schweitzer that the road which "leads through 'metaphysics' is a fatal error which has already enjoyed too long a span of life in our Western thought," and that "it would be tragic if we renewed its vigor just now." [84] From Altizer to Cox, from van Buren to Novak, we are informed, either explicitly or by innuendo, not only that metaphysics is passé and full of misleading pedantry, but that it has been a positive disservice to our spiritual and intellectual life. For example, Altizer finds Greek metaphysics the major culprit in the corruption of Christianity, for it metaphysicalized the Sacred back out of the world into which it had finally come once and for all in Christ by formulating the doctrine of the resurrection. Cox blames metaphysical thought for absolutizing history and truth, and Hamilton blames it for imprisoning God in the categories of a static theology. And the prejudice is even reflected in Novak's theological venture which deliberately leaves "Maritain and Gilson and even Lonergan behind." Paul van Buren thinks metaphysics is logically and positively for the bliks. The only possible exception is Dewart. It is true he calls for a "dehellenization" of Catholic theology, but he inclines in his reinterpretation of it toward the "transcendental" Thomism of Marechal, Rahner, Marc, and Lonergan.

It would make it easier if we were sure what they mean by metaphysics, or just what *kind* they have in mind. They all equate otherworldliness, transcendent categories, static thought forms, and anything "Absolute" with metaphysics, not to mention anything uselessly abstract and hopelessly unempirical. They all seem to have in mind only one kind of metaphysics— bad. And from the examples they give and the devastating criticism they put forth, who would disagree that it isn't? But the term is vague and tends to become emotive, rather than descriptive, more times than not. As in the case of Schweitzer, one is uncertain whether metaphysics refers to a particular philosophical method, a style of thought, a specific philosophical system or general historic period such as German idealism. As far as I can determine they equate it with blindly speculative, pseudoscientific, semitheological, close-ended, a priori, static, system-building metaphysics. And this is unfortunate, for those of them that do. It shows a lack of awareness of its variety and diversity, and of its more recent trends, as well as a lack of philosophical sophistication about their own claims, speculations, and presuppositions. This is why I have mixed feelings about this prejudice they share: I accept many of their criticisms of metaphysics, while opposing their apparent wholesale rejection of it. I do not think that they need to write the obituary of metaphysics in order to affirm humanity or purify religion.

Unlike the process theologians, who seem more knowledgeable about the importance as well as the limitations of metaphysical thought and have moved toward a more complete, systematic understanding of the complex relationship between nature and man, permanence and change, history and self, God and the world, etc., Schweitzer and the Radical theologians, because of disillusionment with classical Christian metaphysics and impatience with theoretical distractions, turn exclusively toward man and his ethico-socio-politico participation in the concrete world without the burden (and benefit) of ontological considerations.

A strange thing is that Schweitzer, who was not naïve about philosophy and what he was attempting to accomplish with rational thought, *does* involve himself in a kind of descriptive metaphysical reflection. Clark is correct when he says: "Although Schweitzer does not work out a *total* world-view based on metaphysical speculation, he certainly does emerge with a more rational hypothesis about 'the whole' than many of his anti-metaphysical comments might imply." [85] (I wonder if the same comment could not be made about most of the Radical theologians?) "Schweitzer's philosophy is a carefully thought out attempt to piece together those facts and experiences which seem to be authentic into an ordered pattern of meaning which is held to be valid for all men"—and this is just the aim and *modus operandi* of that discipline which we call metaphysics.[86] Indeed, as I felt years ago, his discussions of the "will-to-live" lead toward a panentheistic view as found in Whitehead, Hartshorne, Cobb, and Teilhard de Chardin. Clark also detects this and even makes a few provocative comparisons as to where and how Schweitzer and Whitehead, for example, seem in agreement.[87]

The third similarity is the role and importance of ethics in their theological approaches. I am not referring to the obvious fact that as Christian theologians they naturally would extol the importance of the life and ethic of Jesus; it is the crucial importance that the ethical plays in their understanding of man. The ethical is for them not only a set of principles or practical guides to action. It has a broader dimension and deeper *sign*-ificance: it becomes a method of illumination and a source of insight into the very meaning of existence. At the least, it is the way that leads to the heart of the theological arena and its central epiphanies. To humanize the world through the secular epiphany of the incarnate Word, or through love in action, or being a man beside others, or a concerted search for justice through political engagement in the secular city, or through the search for understanding, or reverence for life is not only fulfilling the law of the Christian man, it is the method of uncovery of a fuller comprehension of the nature of the Sacred. Like Schweitzer, they think in the ethical rather than the theological idiom; they prefer the "hard march through ethics" to the devious retreats through theology; and hence their concentration has shifted from apologetics and hermeneutics to "the shape and quality of our lives." [88]

One of the key passages that signaled and pumped along this shift in contemporary theology was written by Bonhoeffer in one of his last letters:

Our relation to God is not a religious relationship to a supreme Being, absolute in power and goodness, which is a spurious conception of transcendence, but a new life for others, through participation in the Being of God. The transcendence consists not in tasks beyond our scope and power, but in the nearest person to hand. God in human form, not, as in other religions, in animal form —the monstrous, chaotic, remote and terrifying—not yet in abstract form—the absolute metaphysical, infinite, etc.—nor yet in the Greek divine-human of autonomous man, but man existing for others, and hence the Crucified.[89]

Twenty-five years earlier Schweitzer wrote:

There is no Essence of Being, but only infinite Being in infinite manifestations. It is only through the manifestations of Being, and *only* through those with which I enter into relations, that my being has any intercourse with infinite Being. . . . By devoting myself to that which comes within my sphere of influence and needs me, I make spiritual, inward devotion to infinite Being a reality and thereby give my own poor existence meaning and richness. The river has found its sea.[90]

And the "sea," which our new life-styles must discover within the expanding demands and idioms of the New Christianity, is reached only by moving out of the swamps of religious superstition and cultural idolatry, past the sandbars of superfluous theological accretions and the back eddies of otherworldliness—beyond the whirlpools of traditional theism.

IV

The Epiphany of Reverence for Life

SCHWEITZER'S RADICAL THEOLOGY ultimately rests upon his analysis of the nature of man-in-the-world, or the will-to-live, for the two most essential aspects of the religious life are combined therein: ethical fervor and cosmic rootedness. The search for world-affirmation leads him to the basic principle of the moral, and the search for a rational and universal ethic leads him to a religious world view or a world yea-saying. The ethical life, always an essential part of every world religion, is not left dangling without support, without its objective counterpart, and the necessity of rootedness is not gained at the expense of intellectual integrity or ethical activity, those acts of spirit which sustain man's high life values in the world. Both are united in a natural way in the concept of Reverence for Life. This was his discovery, his epiphany.

Slowly we crept upstream, laboriously feeling . . . for the channels between the sandbanks. Lost in thought I sat on the deck of the barge, struggling to find the elementary and universal conception of the ethical which I had not discovered in any philosophy. Sheet after sheet I covered with disconnected sentences, merely to keep myself concentrated on the problem. Late on the third day, at the very moment when, at sunset, we were making our way through a herd of hippopotamuses, there flashed upon my mind, unforeseen and unsought, the phrase, "Reverence for Life." The iron door had yielded: the path in the thicket had become visible. Now I had found my way to the idea in which affirmation of the world and ethics are contained side by side! Now I knew that the ethical acceptance of the world and of life, together with the ideals of civilization contained in this concept, has a foundation in thought.[1]

The simple phrase "Reverence for Life" will appear grossly naïve to many, no more than a personal motto quixotically employed to arouse moral sentiment. It also seems beautifully vague, as the Danish theologian P. G. Lindhardt believed when he wrote that Schweitzer's ethic "has aroused much enthusiasm because it can mean anything and everything." [2] And yet, if one is not prejudiced by a phrase and does not burke a deeper study of its multimeanings, its profundity, I believe, becomes apparent.

Schweitzer was aware, of course, that such impressions would arise; he wrote: "It may seem, at first glance, as if Reverence for Life were something too general and too lifeless to provide the content of a living ethic. But thinking has no need to trouble us as to whether its expressions sound living enough, so long as they hit the mark and have life in them. Anyone who comes under the influence of the ethic of Reverence for Life will very soon be able to detect . . . what fire glows in the lifeless expression." [3]

In order to determine whether Schweitzer's thought "hits the mark" or not, it is necessary, first of all, to determine what ideas are contained in his concept of "will-to-live" and what relationship it has to Reverence for Life. Anyone who expects to understand Schweitzer's radical thought must begin here, for it is the key to his whole religious philosophy. It is imperative that the term be closely analyzed. His phenomenology of man offers us a set of experiential tools for opening up a new dialogue between the religious and the secular mind; for Schweitzer biological secular man becomes a possibility for theological discovery and analysis.

A word, first, about the following. Schweitzer does not attempt any thoroughgoing, systematic study of the will-to-live.

Many obscurities and difficulties could have been averted if he had done so, but he did not. I have been obliged to push ahead where his ideas remain vague and inchoate. This is valid, for each of the main divisions of the will-to-live which I discuss are implicit, I find, in his use of the term. Secondly, I have the strong impression that Schweitzer holds to the view that general propositions about the basic features of man and the world are also about God, or the mysterious Life-Force, and that God talk is a special way of speaking about man: it is man seen from the perspective of a cosmic moral relatedness. Theology is psychology, biology, ethics, and philosophical anthropology with a prayer shawl. For example, the will-to-love, or the "instinctive reverence for life," is an authentic aspect of human nature and possesses an ontological character and therefore reveals something about, or has something to do with, what theologians have called "God." Hence the following study is theological in this sense; it is the way contemporary minds "do" theology: they begin with the known, not the unknown; with what is at hand, not with theological puzzles and postulates. Thirdly, what follows will seem at first to have little to do with Radical theology. But before any further comparison or interpretation is possible we have to follow where Schweitzer's thought leads and allow him to speak in his own tongue.

While Freud introduced into psychology what is called the pleasure principle, or the will-to-pleasure; and Adler made us conversant with the role of the will-to-power as a main factor in human behavior; and while, more recently, Viktor Frankl, a one-time Freudian psychiatrist now a psychotherapist, stresses the will-to-meaning,[4] Schweitzer speaks of the will-to-live, which includes all of the above and several other important factors which he believes more adequately account for man's nature.

Though the word is taken primarily as the urge to maintain existence, *Willen zum Leben* in Schweitzer's hands becomes a holophrastic term. It means and represents many things. It includes within it at least three major divisions: the will-to-survival, or self-preservation; the will-to-self-realization; and the will-to-relatedness, or union, with its two forms: the human and the cosmic.

The first points to the struggle for survival. Organisms strive to remain alive and to meet their various physical needs. There is the necessity for air, water, food, sleep, sex, exercise, and shelter. Due to the many exigencies of the physical organism there are the prerequisites of survival to be met. In its prima-facie sense this is what is meant by the will-to-live; it is the first fact that comes to consciousness. "Thus, if we ask, 'What is the immediate fact of my consciousness? What do I self-consciously know of myself, making abstractions of all else, from childhood to old age? To what do I always return?' We find the simple fact of consciousness is this, *I will to live.* Through every stage of life, this is the one thing I know about myself. I do not say, 'I am life'; for life continues to be a mystery too great to understand. I only know that I cling to it. I fear its cessation—death. I dread its diminution—pain. I seek its enlargement—joy." [5]

A closer reading reveals that there is more involved, however, than the urge-to-stay-alive. In the human organism we discover another tendency. This is the will-to-self-realization. Schweitzer uses several terms to describe it: "the craving for perfection," [6] "the will-to-progress," [7] "the will to the realization of ideals," [8] "the will to civilization." [9] There is a difference between this and the will-to-survive, for we can make a distinction between the mere will to stay alive, the ability of adaptation, and the surge of energy within the organism which strives to bring it to its fulfillment. This will-to-self-realization is instinctive in the single-celled organisms, the insects, and most of the animal kingdom. But as we ascend the scale, the more highly organized forms of life, which possess more and more specialized organs of sense and response, come to depend less and less upon blind, instinctive responses. Activity, instead of being unconscious attempts to release energy and relieve tensions by efforts of various kinds, now becomes a conscious process of trial and error, so that the will-to-self-realization eventually comes to depend more upon conscious and cognitive striving than upon instinctive responses. The energy expended by all organisms, directed toward the maintenance and extension of its own life and that of its species, can be spoken of as teleological in this biological sense. But in man we can more truly speak of purposive behavior because of the conscious and intelligent effort involved.

Confining our observations to the human level we discover that not only does man have the ability to be aware of an end in view and the kind of effort necessary to reach it, but in him we reach a higher level of purposive activity altogether. After the particular physical needs of the organism are met, there are other urges and desires within the human personality that must be recognized. These are tendencies which no simple or single physical function of the organism can satiate. Because the human being possesses self-awareness, memory, intelligence, imagination, and the ability to abstract meanings from signs and symbols in communication, the fulfillment of his latent needs will need be different from that of other organisms. Indeed, the will-to-self-realization reaches a new level, so to speak, in man and becomes capable of reflection upon itself and of rational control and guidance. This new syndrome of powers brings versatility, subtler manipulation, greater adaptability, and more complex levels of expression.

This is a mixed blessing, however. The acquirement of a wider range of consciousness and the departure from automatic, adaptive responses brings with it a dreadful freedom. Man's higher intelligence makes him less a slave to his environment and the rigid routes of primitive biological habits, but there is a concomitant loss of instinctive certainty and he must go groping toward means, with the new acquirement of aesthetic, moral, and rational insight, which must fulfill ends in keeping with the new urges of his will-to-self-realization.

Thus there appears to be at work within man a latent drive,

or urge, or will to realize his potentialities, to become more than he is at any one particular moment. This predilection is difficult to pinpoint and harder to explain; but it is too prevalent to ignore. The very fact that man has ascended to more efficient levels of doing, knowing, making, and willing throughout the rhythmic course of his history is evidence not only that he strives to satisfy and satiate his physical desires but that he also has a strong urge to realize those other qualities of his nature reflected in his search for goodness, beauty, and truth. "In us beings who can move about freely and are capable of pre-considered, purposive activity, the craving for perfection is given in such a way that we aim at raising to their highest material and spiritual value both ourselves and every existing thing which is open to our influence." [10]

The will-to-self-realization, however, may not be that obvious to us, for it assumes many forms: it may purposely be ignored; it may exist in a distorted manner that works toward its own destruction; it may be waylaid by fortuitous circumstances and pass into hidden hibernation; it may even atrophy. Yet it can be detected in the most amazing expressions in art, music, science, religion, philosophy, and all the other creative areas of life. These human expressions may be accounted for in numerous and sundry ways by the various sciences. But submerged and running broadly beneath all these secondary explanations moves a force that can only be equivocally expressed by such terms as will-to-self-realization. "How this striving originated within us, and how it has developed, we do not know, but it is given with our existence. We must act upon it, if we would not be unfaithful to the mysterious will-to-live which is within us." [11]

The third element of the will-to-live, which makes up part of our nature, is the will-to-relatedness. It could perhaps be included under the will-to-self-realization, yet Schweitzer speaks of the "will-to-love," [12] the "ethical will within us," [13] the yearning of the will-to-live "to arrive at unity with itself, to become Universal," [14] and the desire to experience "union with the infinite will in which all life is one." [15] This broadens the character of self-realization considerably, thus another division of the will-to-live is necessary. I have refrained from labeling it in the above manner, first, because of the sentimental connotations and misconceptions that arise over the word "love," and, secondly, because of the dubiousness of such an unadulterated "ethical will" in man which is suggested. The broader term that I have chosen, which includes love, in all its forms, and the vestigial source of ethical will, seems more apropos.

The will-to-relatedness I divide into two parts: the *human*, or active, which is characterized by the desire for personal and social solidarity; and the *cosmic*, or passive, which is expressed in the desire for reunion and rootedness.

The proclivity for human relatedness exhibits itself in two ways: namely, man's gregariousness and his need to belong, which issues in the rise of societies and solidary interests, and man's need to love and be loved, which issues in ties of friendship, sympathetic concern, and more responsibility. The former is the more expedient and practical type of relatedness; the latter are the more ideal types, which aim toward personal relationship and true community.

The urge to cosmic relatedness also expresses itself in two ways: namely, the need for union in the wider, more universal sense, which issues mainly in man's religious expressions signified partly by his search for the holy, or whole-ness, and at-one-ment; and the will-to-meaning, which issues in man's intellectual quests for truth concerning the nature of things and his possible relation to them.

"Our thought seeks ever to attain harmony with the mysterious spirit of the Universe. To be complete, such harmony must be both active and passive. That is to say, we seek harmony both in deed and in thought." [16]

Schweitzer begins his analysis of the will-to-live with what he calls the "primary axiom of consciousness." The "most immediate and comprehensive fact of consciousness" is: "I am life which wills to live, in the midst of life which wills to live." [17] This is, for him, not an "ingenious dogmatic formula" like Descartes' *cogito ergo sum* which led modern philosophy "irretrievably on the road to the abstract" and modern thought into a perilous bifurcation of the world.[18] It is an axiom more fundamental and concrete; it is simple, direct—an initial awareness of existence. "Day by day, hour by hour, I live and move in it. At every moment of reflection it stands fresh before me." [19] Whatever else man is conscious of, he is conscious of a peculiar flow of impulses within and of a constant continuum of happenings about him. The exact *raison d'être* of these manifestations he does not know, but he forms a conception of them by analogy with the will-to-live which is within himself. In this way his theoretical knowledge of the world passes over into experience of the world. Such elemental knowledge unites him with an inner dimension of all events. "From within outwards," says Schweitzer, "it puts me in relation to the world by making my will-to-live feel everything around it as also will-to-live." [20]

It will become obvious, if it has not already, that though Schweitzer begins with a primary act of human consciousness he does not confine the will-to-live to human life. It is true it is used as a descriptive term to express the manifold operations of human beings, as well as signifying single traits with the individual person (as when he says, "To analyze reason fully would be to analyze the will-to-live"); [21] but it also on occasion can be taken to be synonymous with what is meant by "life," referring to all the growing and living things that populate the earth. Not only does it signify all animate, but it applies to inanimate events as well, viz., the will-to-live is found even "in the flowering tree, in the strange forms of the medusa, in the blade of grass, in the crystal." [22] And further, it also symbolizes the creative force within these things and everything that exists. By means of my will-to-live "my existence joins in pursuing the aims of the mysterious universal will of which I am a manifestation." [23] Everything, including man, is part of an amazing and enigmatic enterprise.

To an oversophisticated age such as ours, which distrusts the simple and finds answers only in the highly specialized and complex, beginning with an axiom so vague as "I am will-to-live" will seem most naïve. How does Schweitzer expect to extrapolate a solid world view and ethic from such a passé vitalism with Schopenhauerian overtones? Nurtured so long and so exclusively on an empiricostatistical fare, such talk about will and inner forces and innate drives and cosmic spirit will be most distasteful, if not unpalatable, to present tastes. But Schweitzer's main insights will slip away if we become bogged down in carping about his nineteenth-century terms, or entangled in pedantic debates about free will versus determinism, innate versus acquired characteristics, heredity versus environment, vitalism versus behaviorism, and so forth. It is true that there may be nothing startlingly new in what he has to say about the first two aspects of the will-to-live, but it is in the third in which his major contribution comes to light, and we can better understand, particularly in regard to what he is trying to do, the reasons he believes it is so illuminating.

The first part of Schweitzer's primary axiom of consciousness, "I am life that wills to live," characterizes the individual; its corollary part, "amidst other life that wills to live," describes the interpersonal character of the organism and the social milieu in which it functions. The will-to-relatedness is actually a part of our urge-for-survival. How is this? Man is intimately tied to his kind and utterly depends upon others for survival. Indeed, he would not be "human" without social interaction. This is obvious.

Yet Schweitzer finds there is another factor that appears in the sheer contingent relation of one organism to another. Nature compels us, he says, to sympathize with other life and to aid it, for it makes life originate in life, "which for a time needs our help in order to be able to exist." In this manner a solidarity between our life and other life is created. "In the very fibers of our being, we bear within ourselves the fact of the solidarity of life." [24]

How much deeper does Wilhelm Stern go than did Darwin! According to Darwin, experience of the never ceasing, universal danger to existence produces in the end nothing but the herd-instinct, which holds together creatures of the same species. According to Stern, there is developed by the same experience a kind of solidarity with everything that lives. The barriers fall. Man experiences sympathy with animals, as they experience it, only less completely with him. Ethics are not merely something peculiar to man, but, in a less developed form, are to be seen also in the animal world as such. Self-devotion is an experience of the deepened impulse to self-preservation.[25]

Man's predilection for concerned relatedness is more than the result of a herd instinct, expedient selfishness, or social conditioning. An instinctive reverence for life is part of his will-to-live. When it is reflected upon man he realizes that his own self-realization is jeopardized unless he gives full expression of this concern for all life. He needs to give, as well as receive, mutual aid and love. Only in this way can he find a relatedness that preserves the integrity of all parties involved and allows him to be a part of a mutually sharing community in which his unique potential as a person can be expanded. Only in this way is he able to move from thinghood to ego-hood to the freedom and integrity of personhood.

If through indifference and ignorance we neglect this aspect of our natures, a callousness develops, and we insulate ourselves from that sensitivity which we have in common with other lives. There then results a narrowing of the range of values, and we alienate ourselves from other lives and from an understanding of them and eventually from ourselves. There results a loss of humanity; and this is no mere metaphor, for it means that psychic damage results. This is what gives a categorical character to the moral "ought," its imperative comes from a different direction: instead of through my selfish will-to-survive or personal will-to-self-realization, it comes from a reverence for life that seems beyond me in the midst of the world (though in reality it is still I who feel the need and make the command).

Schweitzer is quite explicit about ethics being rooted in man's nature. Reverence for life, he writes, "does not need to make any pretensions to high titles or noble-sounding theories to explain its existence. Quite simply, it has the courage to admit that it comes about through physiological make-up. *It is given physically*. But the point is that it can arrive at the noblest spirituality." [26]

Why, if this is so, is the sentiment of reverence for life, or the will-to-love, so ridiculed, and the possibility of true altruistic acts even denied?

As when a person from some psychotic disorder believes he cannot walk, and eventually cannot because his limbs have atrophied, so modern man is losing his ability for moral concern by convincing himself that love is basically egoistic; that altruism is selfishness in disguise, that the natural sentiments of pity and sympathy are signs of weakness, and that the main aim of every "enlightened" ego is the cultivation of a clever will-to-power. Schweitzer stands opposed to such beliefs; he strives to awaken once again the spirit of humanity, to reestablish a confidence in the moral potential of man. While for most the will-to-live is only capable of becoming an egregious will-to-power (and hence needs close heteronomous watching), for Schweitzer it is capable of transforming itself into a powerful will-to-love-and-justice through reverence for life.

We must not, however, be naïve as to what Schweitzer is implying about man's natural moral proclivities. John Middleton Murry and others have not fully understood Schweitzer on this point. They have accused him of making "an enormous leap" from a "primitive and primary 'will-to-live' . . . a warring egoism into a reverence for all life, which is claimed to be a necessity of thought." [27] The will-to-live is not transmuted automatically into an altruistic will-to-love by any means. The warring ego is not replaced. There is given in our natures both a will-to-self-preservation *and* a will-to-love. And more often

than not they clash. That man has a certain nature does not
ipso facto mean that all his potentialities will be completely
and properly realized. Man's proclivity toward pity and sympathy and concern for others is not lifted to a functional and
ethical level without effort, will, and understanding. Mr.
Murry should have said that the will-to-live *can* and does *at
times* "assume the form of the will-to-be-ethical." [28] But it does
so in no simple nor automatic, magical way. Seaver correctly
vindicates Schweitzer's position by stating, "It is *not* true that
Schweitzer's ethical mysticism is derived from the experience
of vitalism; it is derived from the *reflection* of rational man
upon that experience." [29] It is the task of thought, speaking out
of the natural impulses of pity and sympathy, to refine and to
raise the will-to-live to the level of intelligent self-devotion or
moral concern. "This reverence for life is given as an element
of my will-to-live and becomes clearly conscious of itself *only*
as I *reflect* about my life and about the world." [30]

To those, like Clark, who criticize Schweitzer for his naïve
Rationalist's faith in reason and its ability to turn man's will-
to-live into a will-to-love and maintain it as an ethical force
in society without the aid of something else to do the trick like
"a prior commitment," let me say, first, that the will-to-live is
not just "the brute instinct of self-preservation," [31] but contains also, albeit inchoately, a will-to-human-concern; and,
secondly, that the experience of reverence has not been adequately taken into consideration as a factor in the whole undertaking. Reason is tempered with, and guided by, reverence,
and as Professor Everett points out, this is different from faith
and commitment. "To be committed to life is different from
having reverence for it. To revere is to discover something
awesome and holy, something that grasps and holds the person. This is not intellectual commitment, it is not emotional
attachment, it is not something once felt that can be denied;
it is a final and unconditional religious act. It is not even an
act of faith or of blind obedience." [32] Schweitzer's reason is a
specially sensitive kind of reflection that looks on man and the

self out of the experience of reverence for life.

Man can partially fulfill his need for relatedness by enter-ing into primary relationships and by belonging as an accepted member of a social group. But it cannot be completely fulfilled in this manner, for he yearns for a wider, more universal re-latedness. He seeks to become united in a meaningful way with the world at large. This is accomplished: either through religious worship, sacred ritual, mystical experience, and even, at times, through aesthetic communion with nature; or by in-tellectually understanding the world through systems of theo-retical knowledge. Man's curiosity and thirst for knowledge are part of his will-to-relatedness, for knowing is a type of relatedness. As Schweitzer noted: "We could not be satisfied to belong to the universe only as physical beings; we wanted to belong to it also as spiritual critics. We aimed at our spirit be-coming one with the spirit of the universe." [33] Whatever man considers "the spirit of the universe" to be, he tries to under-stand it, to be part of it, whether by revelatory illumination, intuition, reason, creative imagination, symbolic constructs, or by direct involvement and practical action. He tries to become united with the universe in a way that will, if not reveal its essential nature, at least give his life meaning.

Viktor Frankl, who like Bonhoeffer was a prisoner in a Nazi death camp during World War II, believes that the "will-to-meaning" is the truest expression of man's nature. He defines it as a deep-seated striving of man for ultimate meaning, a meaning to be fulfilled by him and him alone. In his opinion, "man is neither dominated by the will-to-pleasure nor by the will-to-power, but by a will-to-meaning." [34] "This search for a meaning to existence and one's own existence is man's most primary concern." [35] It is something that cannot be unmasked or debunked as a so-called "secondary rationalization," "re-action formation," or mere "sublimation," he says, for we are confronted here with what is genuine in man.

Schweitzer, I am sure, would be sympathetic with Frankl's analysis of the will-to-meaning and would agree that it is a reality and an essential aspect of the human being. This is the reason I have included it in the third division of the will-to-live. Many of Schweitzer's statements concerning the will-to-live reflect this concern.

There are several curious things about this feature of man. First, just as man's will-to-love can be neglected or corrupted, which often leads to grave consequences, so too with the will-to-meaning. Frankl states that if man fails to give his life a meaning worth living and suffering for, and "this most human demand" remains unfulfilled or frustrated, then an anxiety results that runs the chance of becoming pathological. It may retreat into a fanatical form of relatedness, e.g., utopianism or ascetic otherworldly mysticism, or an egregious will-to-power, or a primitive will-to-pleasure. All are frenetic ways man has of wringing a meaning from the world at all costs, or more accurately, of repressing the demands of his will-to-meaning. Afraid of his inner void he escapes into these other modes of behavior, which for a time give him a false sense of security and accomplishment. But then the life of pleasure, the power of personal aggrandizement, and even social respectability, become tattered garments that do not conceal his naked anxiety. Today, "what we can observe in a majority of people is not so much the feeling of being inferior or less valuable than others, but the feeling that life no longer has any meaning. An existential vacuum threatens him. A nihilism which denies that Being has a meaning." [36] Such a state of the soul—which seems more prevalent today than in former times—ought not to be taken as a sign of disease or abnormalcy, Frankl insists, it ought to be seen as a basic feature of the human condition and dealt with accordingly. Instead of ignoring the will-to-meaning, or trying to exorcise it with Freudian cures, or "drowning it in a sea of tranquilizers," [37] we must try to stimulate it and give it proper guidance.

The will-to-meaning can become misdirected and work toward its own undoing, in a second way. This comes about when man overemphasizes the passive form of relatedness to the neglect of the active. We have witnessed it in the past fifty years or so that instead of becoming *more* meaningfully related to the world, man's knowledge and intellectual pursuits have progressively alienated him from the world and the centers of meaning that once made his life significant and purposeful, they have increased his anxiety, not lessened it; have failed more, not less, to meet the demands of his will-to-meaning. The natural solidarity of man and world has been ruptured. He is no longer a bold mariner, but a seasick sailor who has fallen on his oars in despair feeling the futility of rowing any further. He sees only an unending horizon. He drops the tiller from his hands and drifts aimlessly with the currents, moving further away from any haven of meaning.

How did this come about? It came about, partly because modern man thought he could enter into relatedness with the world only passively, that is, only intellectually. His success in accurately describing, measuring, calculating, manipulating, and predicting natural phenomena as a scientific spectator gave him confidence that such an approach was entirely sufficient, not only for understanding reality, but for knowing how to live meaningfully in the world. In this manner the quest for relatedness became sidetracked into a stockpiling of information facts and technological techniques that were not only mute about the richness of the qualitative aspects of human life, but eventually worked toward the discrediting of those valuable insights and meanings which were basic to an optimistic world view. Such a tack has misled contemporary man into a false relatedness, not only with his fellowmen, but, many feel, with the essential character of existence itself. And the deception continues.

Schweitzer insists that cosmic relatedness fails if it becomes abstract and seeks only intellectual union. Modern man has sought to fulfill his will-to-meaning solely in this way; but such attempts lure him farther from contact with satisfactory rootedness, his will-to-relatedness has been deviated from its course into the sands of abstract speculation and the underbrush of knowledge facts where it has evaporated. As man cannot belong to the universe only as a physical object, so he cannot be related meaningfully to it only intellectually as a calculating machine. Knowledge of external relations is not enough; he also needs knowledge of internal *relatedness*.

Does this mean that, the more man knows about the world, the more frustrated and alienated he becomes? No; for as we have seen, it is *how* one knows that is important. I begin with the immediate and obvious fact of existence—that I am will-to-live, and that, secondly, all about me are manifestations of the same will. In this awareness my *theoretical* knowledge of the physical world passes over into *experiential* knowledge. I feel a kinship with all existence, not abstractly but existentially. If then I seek, out of this natural reverence for life, to be united with all Life, I fulfill, at the same time, both my will-to-human- and will-to-cosmic-relatedness; I am rooted intellectually as well as spiritually; passively as well as actively. I experience not only a social solidarity but a cosmic relatedness; hence a world-relatedness, and a more living one, is gained through a life-relatedness. "Ethics alone can put me in true relationship with the universe by serving it, cooperating with it; not by trying to understand it. It is through community of life, not community of thought, that I abide in harmony with that Will," i.e., "the Creative Will whence all life emanates." [38]

Does not Schweitzer violate his own prejudice against nature philosophies and metaphysics when he speaks of a "Creative Will" or "the mysterious will-to-live which is in all things"? Is he not contradicting himself when he says at one place that ethics "cannot be conceived as being merely a nature happening which continues itself in man," [39] and then at another says, "By its means (i.e., reverence for life) my existence joins in pursuing the aims of the mysterious universal will of which I am a manifestation"? [40] Yes and no. He does break the self-imposed limitation on his thought by enlarging the circle of the will-to-live to include "everything," but only the first two divisions, only with regard to Nature exhibiting a will-to-maintain and actualize itself. The attempt to explain all animate matter by a single universal principle, as Schweitzer does, leads invariably to life's inexorable connection with the universe which engendered it. Though one cannot plausibly speak of inanimate matter as possessing a "will" of its own, or a "self," still one can attempt to come to a more accurate (operational) explanation of the whole through analogical reasoning. And this is what Schweitzer has done; he reads analogically into the world the striving and willing which are found within life, and takes a step toward basing his new religion upon a nature philosophy. But as he even admits, it is an "elemental," open-ended nature philosophy that can do us no harm. He compares it with the "magnificently unfinished" nature philosophy of Goethe, whom he greatly admired.[41] Goethe, he writes:

strives to reach an ethical conception of the universe, but admits to himself that he cannot succeed. So he does not venture to attribute a meaning to nature. To life, however, he desires to attribute a meaning. He seeks it in serviceable activity. . . . To the conviction that activity provides the only real satisfaction in life, and that therein lies the mysterious meaning of existence, he gives expression in *Faust* as something which he has laboriously gained during his pilgrimage through existence and to which he will hold fast, without being able to explain it completely.[42]

In the same way Schweitzer concedes that he finds a struggle for survival and a will-to-self-realization in nature, but as to finding a will-to-relatedness or the ethical will in nature and the universe he fails. There is a serious severance in the schematic stages of the will-to-live. He expresses this basic disunity by the word *Selbstentzweiung,* or "division of life against itself." [43] This is the "dilemma of the will-to-live." [44] "Our will-to-live has to accommodate itself to the inconceivable truth that it is unable with its own valuable convictions to discover itself again in the manifold will-to-live which is seen manifested in the world." [45]

According, then, to what may be called Schweitzer's principle of *Selbstentzweiung*, it is impossible to read into the world an optimistic *telos* or ethical purpose. The will-to-live cannot be traced alike from the lowest level of Being to the highest in all respects, for "high up in the ascent it breaks off with chasms ahead." The first and second aspects of the will-to-live give us a firm tie with the universal manifestations of the will-to-live, but when we approach the place where we may validly find ethical purposive activity in the *world at large* with which we may identify ourselves, the facts fail us.

The bitter disappointment in failing to attain an optimistic, religious view founded on knowledge of the universe has thrown many into pessimistic inactivity, or into a pose of arrogant defiance; or it has forced others to allow their willing to overpower their thinking, and an optimistic world view to be projected in the face of facts to the contrary. For Schweitzer such extremes are neither valid nor necessary. The division may be healed by moral commitment and the mystical outlook of reverence for life. "The root-idea of my theory of the universe is that my relation to my own being and to the objective world is determined by reverence for life." [46] We can be honest about what we know concerning the universe and still find the required world view. We can build securely upon what we know about the Life-Force as it expresses itself in man. He who tries to understand the world and to discover the highest elements of his nature duplicated there, says Schweitzer, "is a ship-wrecked castaway; the will-to-live which gets to know itself is a bold mariner." [47]

The phrase "Reverence for Life" may now be better understood. Instead of an expletive moral maxim, it takes on a significance hitherto overlooked. It is not just an ethic; it includes also an insight into the nature of things. That is why Schweitzer can say: "And this ethic, profound, universal, has the significance of a religion. It *is* religion." [48] Suddenly, while straining against the "iron door," which barred him from discovering the basic principle of the moral, and stumbling about in the dense "thickets" of pessimism searching for a path that would lead him toward world affirmation, there flashed upon his mind a phrase that fused together the is and the ought, fact and value, nature and spirit, God and man, in one epiphanic insight. That it does this can be seen, partially, by its descriptive as well as its prescriptive function in the following meanings of the term.

First, as a biological expression it means I am an urge to survival, I instinctively affirm my *own* life by reason of the obvious fact that I will to live. Schweitzer calls this an "instinctive reverence for life." With every beat of one's heart there is an unconscious affirmation of life within us.

Secondly, I also consciously revere my own life, for as a self-aware organism I seek to develop and enlarge my own powers. Proper self-development, of course, comes only when I move from a simple to a deepened self-affirmation, from an instinctive to an enlightened self-regard. Thus "reverence for life" lays an obligation upon me to discover what it means to esteem oneself and to realize one's human potentialities properly. As Eric Fromm and many others have pointed out, one cannot love others without first knowing what it means truly to love oneself. A lack of reverence for ourselves makes us our own worst enemies. This meaning of Schweitzer's term is often completely overlooked.

Thirdly, the phrase signifies the third aspect of the will-to-live. I have a natural proclivity toward relatedness and concern with other lives. I am also will-to-love. I desire to enter into and be part of others' wills-to-live. This describes my nature as accurately as my tendency to fight to stay alive or to seek my own happiness. It is that phase in the development of the human being when the tendential potentiality of regard and concern for others is refined and enhanced.

In the fourth place, "reverence for life" means a concern, not only for my own life or for other human life, but for *all* life whatsoever. Regardless of how fleeting, it is there, and all of us feel it from time to time. There is a mysterious tie with the will-to-life which we perceive in all animal, bird, insect, and even plant life. This gives Schweitzer's ethic its totally inclusive nature when he moves from the purely descriptive to the prescriptive use of the phrase. Schweitzer makes the revolutionary statement that future ages will look back upon our period of history with amazement for our neglect to include such life within the sphere of moral behavior, just as we look back in disbelief at those who once regarded the colored peoples as less developed forms of human life and justified their use of them as fair game in shooting expeditions or as slaves to die in exhausting labor.

Giving ontological status to the word "Life," or "Will-to-Live," the phrase *"Erfurcht vor dem Leben"* becomes a capsulized expression for Schweitzer's "mysticism of reality." It signifies a reverence or veneration for the Universal Will or Reality in which all things are grounded. Through this attitude (frame of mind, allegiance) man seeks to become united with it, and thus strives to overcome the estrangement and split (*Selbstentzweiung*) which he finds between nature and spirit, matter and mind. Schweitzer is referring here to man's proclivity toward unity or cosmic rootedness which is manifested empirically in man's religious and quasi-religious attempts to "cosmicize" the world,[49] and is found in his thirst for comprehensiveness or comprehension of himself within the Totality.

Lastly, in the obvious meaning of the term, "reverence for life" serves as an ethical admonition or moral maxim by stressing what one *ought* to do. This is its prescriptive function.

It is interesting that Schweitzer is able to combine in a natural way the "is" and the "ought" in one expression. (This should intrigue philosophers who consider this problem one of the unsolvable riddles in ethical theory.) Clark's comment shows how this is possible. "Schweitzer absorbed from Georg Simmel a conviction that the potential 'oughtness' of the essential self is just as real as the actual 'is-ness' of the existing self. . . . The finite will-to-live already has a built-in definition of what self-perfection involves, and the whole point of elemental thinking is to clarify the vision of the essential self so that it may become even more closely approximated in existence." [50] So each of the descriptive meanings has, at the same time, its prescriptive overtone: I instinctively revere my own life—I *ought* to revere myself more highly; I am a self-realizing organism—I *ought* to develop my potential as a person in the highest manner possible; I have a natural tendency toward concern for others—I *ought* to love others and devote myself to them more; I have a natural kinship with all living things—I *ought* to show more concern and tenderness toward them; I have a natural tendency toward rootedness and world-relatedness—I *ought* to seek to become united through religious philosophy and action with the mysterious Universal Will in which *all* Being is grounded. Thus Schweitzer's moral "ought" springs out of the very heart of an analysis of the nature of man-in-the-world, and is not one pragmatically and legalistically propagated *ab extra*.

The puzzling excitement of Schweitzer over his illuminatory experience is further understood when we realize that it also solved for him all the stringent requirements he set down for an adequate ethical theory.

What are these? The first we have already discussed: a complete ethic according to Schweitzer must stand in an effective relation to life and the world as a whole, i.e., it must have a world view.[51] If it does not, it is groundless, and loses in perspicacity, inclusiveness, and universality. It is like trying to walk with only one leg. Ethics cannot stand alone, it must be joined with a view of existence in a natural and dynamic way. Secondly, a valid ethic must be world- and life-affirming. An ethic of life- and world-negation that tries to live in an atmosphere of pessimism, whether it is enlightened or not, suffocates.[52] Thirdly, it must be active and not only passive. A passive ethic concerns itself with only the perfecting of the self (which Nietzsche, whom Schweitzer praises, strongly stressed), while a true ethic must lend itself to the altruistic relation of man to man.[53] Fourthly, it must combine these two, i.e., the ethic of self-realization and of self-devotion, in a forceful and natural way.[54] Fifthly, it must be universal and not limited to setting the ends of its action only in the relation of man to man. It must encompass *all* forms of life.[55] Next, it must not regard its basic principle as coming from the expediencies of social enculturation as if ethics were a solely social phenomenon whose maxims worked from the group level down. Its moral precepts must come from reflection upon the essential nature of man and his proper perfecting upward into society so as to help it keep its moral balance and even lift it to higher planes of decision and action.[56] And, lastly, it must be "absolute," by which Schweitzer means unlimited concern unhindered by rules of expediency.[57] Schweitzer's ethic is absolute not in its origins, but in its goal or allegiance; it does not lay down any specific rules for each situation, it sets no minimum or maximum limits to what we must do, it simply tells us that we ought to have unlimited responsibility for all life that comes within our reach. This is similar to Fletcher's situational ethic which stresses that only one thing is intrinsically good, namely, love.

These are the formidable demands of an adequate ethic which Schweitzer sets for himself. Whether he succeeds in meeting them is something else; but that he *thought* he succeeded, with his ethic of Reverence for Life, is the point at hand. Anyone who has been involved in the intricacies of ethical theory will understand the enthusiasm of a person who believes he has formulated *the* "basic principle of the moral"!

Parenthetically it might be said here that even though these demands help us to appreciate the particular problems with which Schweitzer personally became involved, many of the so-called requirements will seem inappropriate and misleading, particularly to the ethicist whose interests lie in another direction and who finds a plethora of ethical complexities apart from this list of strange criteria which seem only to add to the confusion. Many will express doubts as to whether they are legitimate demands; and others will maintain that even if they are crucial, it is doubtful whether they can be substantiated. Also there may be no such thing as *the* basic principle of the moral, implying that there is a single, pervading quality or characteristic inherent in all moral attitudes or acts. And again, what Schweitzer demands may be only the result of his search to find satisfactory answers to a personal philosophy of life. This last point has been stressed with singular determination by John M. Murry, who believes that Schweitzer's whole religious philosophy is the abortive outcome of his straining to justify his emotional dedication to Jesus and a life of sacrifice, by changing it, in good eighteenth-century fashion, from a compulsiveness of his emotional life to a compulsiveness of thought.

Though a critical analysis of each of the above requirements lies beyond the scope of this book, a mention of Schweitzer's solution to one of the problems will illustrate how he believes his ethic succeeds.

One of the major dilemmas of ethical theory in Schweitzer's eyes is the problem of combining in a logical and realistic way the ethic of self-perfecting and the activist ethic of altruism. There seems to be an impassable barrier erected between them. This does not disturb us a great deal; indeed, we often scientifically shore it up in order to give ourselves an excuse for our immoral acts. If it is true that every act is basically the result of selfishness, viz., the result of always acting, not *as* a self, but *for* a self to the exclusion of everyone else, then not only altruism but morality itself is a farce. But the repeated attempts in the history of thought to relate meaningfully egoism and altruism indicate that the problem is a very real and important one. The various solutions have not been very convincing. Often egoism is foolishly rationalized in hopes that it will serve up, as if by magic, something which is truly moral. Or the ethic of self-realization is maintained while altruism goes begging. As Schweitzer states it, at one time ethics "explains altruism as a refined egoism; at another as something which society forcibly imposes on individuals; at another as

something which it develops in him by education; next . . .
as something which he adopts as one of his convictions on the
ground of the urgent representations of society; or again, as
an instinct which he obeys." [58] None of these explanations
succeeds.

Since both are necessary components of a true ethic, is a
synthesis possible? "Do altruism and the perfecting of the self
belong together in such a way that the one is contained in
the other?" [59] Schweitzer replies, "Yes." Elements of both are
genetically found within the human organism, springing from
the will-to-self-realization and the will-to-human-relatedness.
This gives ethical theory the stable and common basis for both.
However, these tendencies cannot be regarded as instinctive
enough to assure automatic development. It is only in conjunction with intelligence and will and commitment that they are
brought to a moral level of development. "Here one is forced
once more by the problem of the *rôle* which thought plays in
the origin of ethics. It seizes on something of which a prelimi-
nary form is seen in an instinct, in order to extend it and bring
it to perfection. It apprehends the content of an instinct, and
tries to give it practical application in a new and consistent
action." [60] Self-perfecting and self-devotion which are united
vestigially in the will-to-live must be joined by elemental
reason and an act of commitment in order to become ethical.

So if one views the will-to-live as universally found in all
things and if one does not seek to be united with it in a merely
abstract or mystical way, then the realization of oneself, viewed
beneath the aegis of Schweitzer's "mysticism of reality," becomes at the same time effort toward the realization of all will-
to-live, or it becomes self-devotion to others. "To thine own
self be true" is not just poetry, it characterizes the continuity
and mutual dynamic relation of ethical self-realization and altruistic devotion to others. The proper perfecting of the self
is seen by Schweitzer to be an altruistic attitude, since to love
oneself properly is to love (the will-to-live in) others. "The
ethics of sincerity towards oneself passes imperceptibly into

that of self-devotion to others." [61]

For Schweitzer the true source of our highest moral insights and deepest intuitions are dim perceptions of the unitary, creative life-force which flows into the many separate centers of awareness. We are bound together more mysteriously, more intimately than we ever realize; you are in all living beings, and all living beings are in you; the same will-to-live stirs us all. What happens to others, happens to you. You and I and that pelican and this cat are not distinct multiverses, but, in reality, are strangely one. The religious philosophy of Reverence for Life—which is a kind of theological ecology—binds together my life and all life. It magnifies our sensibilites and helps thought formulate for us the basic principle of the moral which is, "It is good to maintain and to encourage life; it is bad to destroy or to obstruct it." [62] It helps break down the barriers between lives upon which egoism, greed, hatred, oppression, and even self-abuse are built; it explains the source of our moral intuitions; it bases the moral "ought" upon the objective "is" without doing violence to either; and it roots a living ethic, and an affirmative, religious world view, in the very nature of things.

Speaking theologically, Schweitzer immanentizes the Sacred into the profane by seeing the Will-to-Reverence for Life, or God, diffused into the world. The creative and moral proclivities of life are mixed with the blind creative-destructive forces in the world. In man the Sacred becomes conscious, and hence the voice of conscience, and begins to infect all life with love. Its epiphany comes in man's reflection upon his destiny and meaning, and in his acts of reverence. The Sacred is real, or becomes actualized, in love between man and man, and all life.

Schweitzer's experience of a Cosmic Will manifested in actual beings could be expressed in Altizer's terminology as "an epiphany of the primordial Totality," or the "Original Sacred" which has been "emptied into the world" and its ethical aspect could be called the "Word," and one could say with Altizer, "The Word is active and real *only* in the profane reality of a fallen history." [63] But, of course, Schweitzer has no such elaborate theological schema or rich dialectical language. (Strange, it is Altizer, the American, who is Hegelian—not Schweitzer, the German.) My point is that Schweitzer's conception of the Sacred, or the Word, is one that is completely immanentized into the real, historical world.

The mention of Altizer brings to mind an interesting parallel. Altizer's central vision of the "death of God" concept, which struck him with full force while he was sitting one day in the main library at the University of Chicago reading Erich Heller's Nietzsche and Rilke," was, in his own words, a "radically profane mystical vision" which was "directed to the here and now—to life, flesh, energy." [64] This is similar to Schweitzer's sudden illumination which he experienced traveling by boat up the Ogowe River.

The reader familiar with contemporary religious thought will readily detect some similarities that arise now and then between Schweitzer and the thinkers in the radical tradition. Though it is not my design to make a one-to-one comparison of Schweitzer, even if it were possible, with each of the many radical thinkers past and present, I cannot help briefly mentioning in passing a few glaring similarities between Schweitzer's and Martin Buber's form of mysticism.

We recall that Schweitzer makes a sharp distinction between traditional forms of mysticism, which he calls "abstract mysticism," and his own, which is wholly world-centered, which he calls "ethical mysticism." Buber too was opposed to a mysticism that leads to an absorption of the self into a specious subjectivity by a concentration on one's own spiritual navel, and to an imaginative flight beyond the world into the Absolute. His too was a concrete mysticism which found the true reality in the here and now in the I-Thou relationship. "To look away from the world," he wrote, "or to stare at it, does not help man to reach God; but he who seeks the world in Him stands in His presence." [65] "If you explore the life of things and of conditioned being [the sciences and nature philosophy] you come to the unfathomable; if you deny the life of things and of conditioned being [abstract mysticism and transcendental theologies] you stand before nothingness; if you hallow this life [Reverence for Life] you meet the living God [the Universal Will-to-Love]." [66] Man does not escape the world in the I-Thou relation (Reverence for Life), but is actually more firmly bound up with it in solidarity (ethical mysticism).

God, for Buber, cannot be sought outside or inside the world; he cannot be sought as some *thing* is sought. He who seeks God goes on his way, "but when he has found, his heart is not turned from the world, for everything now meets him in the one event [all is will-to-live]." [67] God, being the Source of all relations, or the Presence of all primal relations, can only be known in actual I-Thou relations, just as Schweitzer insists that the Universal Will-to-Love can only be known as I give myself concretely in ethical love to other wills-to-live. This is their "mysticism of reality."

The radical theology of Reverence for Life may, for many, seem too meager and unfinished to serve as a firm foundation for a religion. To build one's religious destiny upon so simple an outlook is most difficult, if not impossible. Most demand a completed cathedral before they enter with confidence to worship. Certainly, they think, the universe has more to offer than this by way of assuring their faith!

But, according to Schweitzer, if we are honest—and the beginning of all religious faith is honesty—it does not. He openly admits that his religious philosophy is incomplete, but it is enough; it combines the two essential elements of a living religion: ethical fervor and cosmic rootedness. "The surmisings and the longings of all deep religiousness are contained in the ethics of reverence for life. This religiousness, however, does not build up for itself a complete philosophy, but resigns itself to leave the cathedral by necessity unfinished. It is only able to finish the choir. Yet in this, true piety celebrates a living and continuous divine service." [68]

V

The Man Beside Others

WE NOW COME to one of the most intriguing, and instructive, aspects of Schweitzer—the place and significance of Jesus in his life and thought, for Schweitzer too faced the same searching question that Bonhoeffer asked for our time: "How can Christ become the Lord even of those with no religion?" This challenge by Bonhoeffer,[1] which set the stage for a new round of contemporary Christological considerations for the Radical theologians, loomed as a particularly pertinent one also for such a thinker as Schweitzer.

If the theologians of the New Christianity believe that we can no longer speak knowledgeably about God, or that God is hidden or eclipsed, or culturally and religiously dead, or, as some hold, that God is now a useless symbol for a reality that never actually existed, then what becomes of Jesus? How can we speak meaningfully of him? What can his theological function, if any, possibly be? If the Father is absent or dead, then it appears as if the Son is a hoax and our faith is in vain.

Also, if Jesus was not the Son of God, as Schweitzer holds, but was a man, a child of his age, who was even in error about the nature and coming of the Kingdom to which he completely gave his life, and who suffered and died in disillusionment, then it seems impossible to follow him as our Lord and Savior.

But perhaps there is another alternative. Perhaps in our demythologized world Jesus suddenly takes on a new significance—his rightful one—which has hitherto gone unheeded, and he assumes, not in spite of, but *because* of these limitations, a role of far greater import. Such an alternative the Radicals fully affirm.

Hence, despite their turning away from God in order to find man, from the supernatural in order to find the world, from Biblical tradition in order to find secular meaning, they all claim, in one way or another, that Jesus still stands firmly at the center of their faith.

Van Buren, for instance, the strict empiricist, has little patience with things metaphysical, supernatural, divine, or otherworldly, yet he still proclaims as central to his secular "gospel" the semimystical "contagion" of the spirit of Jesus, the catching of which frees all men from their social, intellectual, and psychical chains.[2]

For Vahanian, despite the dead God which contemporary Christianity idolatrously parades, Jesus as the Christ is still capable of fully revealing the living God of the Bible, who continues to be operative as a divine possibility within the arena of human history.[3]

Altizer, seemingly the most radical of all, strictly adheres to the Christian dogma, "God was in Christ." The death of Christ, and hence of God, was a necessary dialectic stage of the Incarnate Word becoming immanentized into the world as part of a cosmic process of constant creative renewal. The eschatological movement of the Kingdom of God, or, as he calls it, the Dialectic of the Sacred, in which Christ plays the major role, is a concept which he finds more primordial and basic than the God concept.[4]

Hamilton still holds to Jesus as Lord—the "man beside others"—and looks to him for inspiration and ethical guidance. The Radical theologian, he says, has a "strange but compelling interest in the figure of Jesus,"[5] and that is why one of his main aims is to try to understand fully "that Jesus who appears in conjunction with the death of God."[6]

Bishop Robinson, however far left he moves in his struggle to be honest to God, remains nevertheless honest to Christ.

Though he rejects the supernaturalistic and the naturalistic interpretations of Jesus—the former because it is incredible and clings to a mythological literalism, and the latter because it abandons "the spirit and power of Jesus," which the Biblical message conveys—he maintains, in the Christological language of Tillich and Bonhoeffer, that because Jesus lived a worldly life and participated in the suffering and powerlessness of God as a man for other men, and because he fully subordinated his existential self to his essential, God-given self, he became transparent for the Ground of Being and hence the full revelation of the Power of the New Being.[7]

For Cox, since man is neither the sole consequence nor the sole cause of social change within history, but combines both, so in a parallel fashion he sees Jesus as both the subject and object of the Kingdom of God. The Kingdom of God is at once a divine and a human act; and since Jesus embodies the Kingdom by combining "both elements of divine initiative and human response," he "remains the fullest possible disclosure of the partnership of God and man in history." [8]

Even Novak, who proposes that Christians should attempt to work out a Christian theology *without* reference to Jesus or Christ [9] (which he himself does), does so, I am convinced, because he believes only in this way can we come to a clearer conception, among other things, of who Jesus is and what his real significance is for us today. His proposal is a sound and a most needed one. Schweitzer would have concurred, I am quite sure, for he too wrote his major theological work without resorting to Christological concepts. Both Novak and Schweitzer, who are in agreement about the importance of philosophy, detected the limitations of the historical Jesus and the exclusivity of the Christ of the Creeds, which warred against Jesus' humanistic and universal appeal, which are their main interests.

In each instance, then, we realize that Jesus remains the magnetic hub of the Radicals' allegiance, the lodestar around which they swing in their search for new theological interpretations and meaningful life-styles for post-Christian man. He endures for them as the paradigm for their expressions of ultimacy.

That this is no less true of Schweitzer goes without saying, it seems, for he speaks of Jesus as the "Lord of our ethical Wills" and the "one truly great man." But in just what ways— and why—he is the Lord of our lives remains on occasion difficult to determine, as we shall see.

To what degree, if any, Schweitzer has had a direct influence on any or all of these men, no one with certainty can tell. But, at least, this can be said: his *Quest of the Historical Jesus* has had a formidable impact upon *all* Protestant thought; secondly, its influence is now more unquestionable than ever since the advent of the *New Quest*,[10] which returns to many of Schweitzer's former insights, and in the appearance of the Theology of Hope,[11] which takes seriously his idea that eschatology and not soteriology was the main motivating force of Jesus and the disciples; thirdly, Schweitzer was one of the first to demythologize the New Testament and reinterpret the significance of Jesus in the light of modern knowledge; and lastly, he shares the freedom of the present scene in his conception of Jesus which bears many resemblances to the Christ portrait of the Radical reformers.

The Radicals, many of them taking their lead from Bonhoeffer, who believed that an "encounter with Jesus Christ" meant a "complete orientation of the human being in the experience" of one "whose only concern is for others," [12] felt the urgent need to move toward the working out of a belief in Jesus as Lord for a secular age. It was a beginning over again from fundamentals for most of them, a definite postorthodox, nontheological, nonreligious rethinking of Christian symbolism and the significance of Jesus. Their orientation is mainly humanistic and ethical, with full emphasis upon Jesus' humanhood and his sacrificial deeds of love. It is also mystical, for there appears a mystical kind of relationship to Jesus (to make up for their lack of interest and acumen in metaphysics, perhaps) in the healthy, thoroughly this-worldly sense similar to Schweitzer's and Buber's "mysticism of reality," which discerns the full Presence of the Sacred only between man and man in I-Thou encounters. This is the true transcendence, according to them—the power that frees all men—and not, as Bonhoeffer had also perceived, the spurious one of a religious relationship to a Supreme Being. It is a mystical involvement in the life of the world in the spirit of "the man for others," "the one in whom Love has completely taken over." [13] "To be a Christian," wrote Bonhoeffer, "does not mean to be religious in a particular way, to cultivate some particular form of asceticism (as a sinner, a penitent, or a saint), but to be a man. It is not some religious act which makes a Christian what he is, but participation in the suffering of God in the life of the world." [14] This quotation of Bonhoeffer links him and Schweitzer and the Radical theologians firmly together in their general outlook on Jesus.

Schweitzer's simple yet powerful understanding of Christianity and what it means to be grasped by the spirituality of Jesus is found in a personal letter he wrote to a music-critic friend, Gustav von Lupke, to whom he was pleading for a more sensitive insight into his decision to become a jungle doctor than most of his friends and acquaintances had the foresight to show:

I hope you will give me the pleasure of showing a deeper insight than most people . . . and that you will find the course I am taking as natural and right as I do myself. For me the whole essence of religion is at stake. *For me religion means to be human, plainly human in the sense in which Jesus was.* In the colonies things are pretty hopeless and comfortless. We—the Christian nations—send out there the mere dregs of our people; we think only of what we can get out of the natives . . . in short what is happening there is a mockery of humanity and Christianity. If this wrong is in some measure to be atoned for, we must send out there men who will do good in the name of Jesus, not simply proselytising missionaries, but men who will help the distressed as they must be helped if the Sermon on the Mount and the words of Jesus are valid and right.

Now we sit here and study theology, and then compete for the best ecclesiastical posts, write thick learned books in order to become professors of theology . . . and what is going on out there where the honour and the name of Jesus are at stake does not concern us at all. And I am supposed to devote my life to making ever fresh critical discoveries, that I might become famous as a theologian, and go on training pastors who will also sit at home, and will not have the right to send them out to this vital work. I cannot do so. For years I have turned these matters over in my mind, this way and that. At last it became clear to me that the meaning of my life does not consist in knowledge or art but *simply in being human and doing some little thing in the spirit of Jesus* . . . "what you have done to the least of these my brethren you have done to me." Just as the wind is driven to spend its force in the big empty spaces so must the men who know the laws of the spirit go where men are most needed.[15]

The kind of Christology that emanates from such a concerned confrontation of the world's pitiable needs and such a simple, direct relationship with Jesus, such as Schweitzer and the new breed of theologians exhibit, is one that strikingly and resolutely shifts its center of gravity from Jesus' pseudo-metaphysical divinity to his human sacrality. The emphasis on Jesus' humanity has always been a part of the church's doctrine of the Trinity, but not in the radical sense in which it now appears. Orthodoxy has been leery of naturalists and liberals who overemphasize Christ's humanity because it believes this inevitably leads to the degrading of Jesus as "a mere human." That this is repellant to the Christian is so for the simple reason that their regard of humans and humanity is so low. Man is a fallen sinner whose only goodness, if it appears at all, is the result of God's grace. From bad theology comes worse psychology. Humanity invariably is taken as the lowest common denominator. The Divine transcendently *separated* from man is regarded as the highest, not the Divine immanently in act with man.

Between the dilemmatic horns of the obscure and effete Jesus of history and the overkerygmatized Christ of faith, there now appears in radical thought Jesus in his spiritual or universal form demanded by the "final age of the spirit," [16] or a world come of age. "The radical Christian rejects both the literal and the historical interpretation of the Bible, demanding instead a pneumatic or spiritual understanding of the Word." [17] Schweitzer speaks of the "spiritualized Jesus" which in his mind is not religiously identifiable with either the dim personage of the first century who was a product of an erroneous Jewish eschatology or the infallible Christ of orthodoxy.

Since Jesus is an inseparable part of his age, Schweitzer warns he must not be lifted out of the past and translated into ours to suit our preconceived notions of him. "As a water-plant is beautiful so long as it is growing in the water, but once torn from its roots, withers and becomes unrecognisable, so it is with the historical Jesus when He is wrenched loose from the soil of eschatology, and the attempt is made to conceive Him 'historically' as a Being not subject to temporal conditions." [18] Then how are we to conceive of him? "Progress in religion consists in its being constantly internalized and spiritualized. In this process it can come to pass that an earlier conviction which was thought to be direct reality later comes to be regarded as truth not in its original sense, but in its spiritual sense. . . . Not with the letter but with the spirit ought our belief preserve a common bond with the past." [19] It is not the historical Jesus nor the deified Christ but the spiritualized Jesus that is acclaimed as the important source of our religious knowledge and inspiration. "It is not Jesus as historically known, but Jesus as spiritually arisen within men, who is significant for our time and can help it. . . . In proportion as we have the Spirit of Jesus we have the true knowledge of Jesus." [20] What Schweitzer means by "true knowledge" here is religious or inspirational knowledge of Jesus. When we study the texts of the New Testament critically and historically, as Schweitzer did, we have true *historical* knowledge of him. But

such knowing is not personal or spiritual; and it is *this* type
of knowing which moves individuals to ethical deeds, and
which is important for our religious life.

It is still an anomaly to most that Schweitzer could push
aside the dross of Biblical interpolations, the gloss of over-
enthusiastic apologetics, the coveted doctrinal adornments of
tradition, and even the modernized versions of liberal Protestantism in order to pour out a few drops of metal of the spiritualized Jesus and still find them precious and soul-gripping.
Most believe he has totally divested Jesus and the Christian
faith of their power; all transcendence is transformed into a
flat secularism by his heretical philosophizing, they say, and
nothing of any inspirational or religious value remains. But,
apparently, for Schweitzer, what remains is not only sufficient
but essential.

It is also strange, as John Wick Bowman noticed, that "we
have, indeed, in Schweitzer the anomaly of a scholar who does
not belong to his own school of thought—not, that is to say, so
far as that school would endeavor to identify its own teachings
with those of the historic Jesus!" [21] That is, historic knowledge
of Jesus will not be sufficient by itself for our religious needs;
indeed, it may at times be an offense to religion. As to the "real"
Jesus, that is, the historic person, Schweitzer finds that the historic facts sketch only a blurred image and hence we shall
never know fully who He is. He remains to us "as One unknown," for "we can find no designation which expresses what
He is for us." [22] But this is not critical, for it is not Jesus
as theologically interpreted, nor known historically as he actually was in his own time (even if this were possible) that
determines his significance or our religious fate, but the power
of the spirit of this "one immeasurably great man" arisen
within us which is essential. Only as we seek to obey his ethical will and enter into the fellowship of the heroic spirit which
streams forth from him, can we come to learn in our own experience and for our own time "Who He is." "The abiding
and eternal in Jesus is absolutely independent of historical

knowledge and can only be understood by contact with His spirit which is still at work in the world." [23]

It might seem highly improbable that one should give unswerving loyalty to even the spirit of a person without knowing "Who He is." But such language is poetic. Jesus is "unknowable" only in the sense that our meager historical knowledge of him is insufficient by itself to meet the demands of our inquisitiveness and religious faith, and that his eschatological outlook and general world knowledge makes his mind forever incommensurable with ours. What facts there are, and indeed, Schweitzer depends upon them as much as anyone, are poignant enough in his mind to stimulate and support a strong ethicoreligious response and a guide for the transformation of our sick culture.

John Charles Cooper, in his book *Radical Christianity and Its Sources*, discusses the reformulation of the significance of Jesus according to several of the Radical theologians. He finds that they move toward what he calls a "functional Christology." It is one "that speaks of the meaning of Christ on the basis of what he did and what he still does through the Spirit," [24] and tries to produce a "theology of full involvement in the needs of the world," [25] one that would "substitute for ordinary theology an exhortation that points in two directions—one toward Jesus as a pattern and example, and the other toward the neighbor and the needs of man. A functional Christology would be the impetus for Christians to make their morality and theology the same thing in their lives." [26] The latter especially constitutes the whole aim of Schweitzer's life and thought: the attempt to make one's theology his morality, and one's morality his theology. Ethics, the ethic of Reverence for Life, *is* religion.

Cooper goes on to characterize a "functional Christology":

It would have to be based on the full human personality of Jesus' life and upon his sacred evaluations of the lives of others—of all others, regardless of mental, physical, moral, economic, or racial condition. A functional Christology would be indeed a reduction of the extent and content of Christian theology, and would need no philosophical basis for itself beyond the everyday more or less scientific biological basis of modern man's own estimation of human life as the ultimate value. No other worlds need be posited, no supernatural order fancifully described, no appeal to faith that flies in the face of reason, but only an appeal to the intuitive awareness of every human being that his life is his most precious possession and his first deduction from this awareness: that the lives of all other creatures must be similarly precious to them.[27]

This, according to Cooper, is the real content of the constructive efforts not only of Altizer (in *The Gospel of Christian Atheism*), but also those of Hamilton, van Buren, and Cox. And then he writes, "In this respect a functional Christology of the type we are suggesting is little different from Schweitzer's doctrine of 'reverence for life,' or from Gandhi's doctrine of Satyagraha, or the 'vow of truth.'"[28] Thus according to Cooper, Schweitzer is a Radical theologian, a truly concerned reformer of the Christian church, for he like Altizer, Hamilton, van Buren, and Cox has only two questions to ask: "(1) What is more sacred than human personality? and (2) What is more sacred than living in love that affirms and preserves our human personality?"[29] Like the others, Schweitzer "holds up a concrete and an intensely personal example, Jesus, and includes a highly experiential element within itself as the basis for the reordering of the church's message and mission."[30]

To the tradition-wrapped mind, of course, this will seem like the bare bones of the once living body of Christology. Theology is collapsed into an anthropology, and Christology into an ethic, no more. Neither the Radicals nor Schweitzer would particularly consider this an indictment, but there is more involved in their Christology, certainly, than moral enthusiasm and commitment to follow the Golden Rule. It must be emphasized that their theologies are not eliminated, they are *fused* with morality; and their morality is fused with a world view, or a mysticism of reality, to use Schweitzer's terms.

A common protest voiced by many radical thinkers for some time now has been that Christianity has too long been hung up on a strictly moralistic interpretation of God's grace, the coming of Christ, and the resurrection, which refers mainly to being saved supernaturally and transformed personally because of fulfilling certain divine duties. The resurrection, for example, is seen only as the moral victory of good over evil. Today Christology attempts to broaden the symbolic significance of the so-called God's act in history. It speaks of the coming of Jesus, his death, and resurrection not as the results of a cosmic moral transaction, but as revealing a new being, a new life, a new dimension within the world. The functional Christology of the Radicals and Schweitzer is not the good-man theory of Jesus revived, in other words. It emphasizes more the creative than the soteriological, more the healing and saving capabilities within man and history instead of beyond man and history, more emphasis upon the here and now instead of the then and when. Besides the Good, the power of the True and the Beautiful are also revealing present possibilities. Man is saved in multiple ways, not just morally; he is healed by the alchemy of aesthetic forms and truths that set him free. Such a Christology, no longer tied to a Semitic, apocalyptic, redemptive schema, enlarges the potential interpretation of the role and work of Jesus as the bearer of the New Life. He becomes a freeing agent in our midst, not just another moral example. In him the immanent Sacred, or the Universal Will-to-Love, or the Ground of Being, or the Reality of the Future, is present in such a way that men's lives can now be transformed into their full potential: morally, intellectually, and aesthetically.

Schweitzer shares with the Radicals the particular attributes of a "functional Christology," as characterized by Cooper, and his general orientation toward the problem is similar. But, of course, there are differences, not only between himself and Radicals, but among the Radicals themselves.

And again, I must caution against overgeneralizing the whole issue. Altizer, Hamilton, Cox, van Buren, Fletcher, *et al.* have their own varying approaches and solutions to the Christological problem, which are not always readily available for easy comparison. Their individual differences must always stand consciously, if not conspicuously, in the background of such a study as this. As to Schweitzer, we may well note now some distinguishing features which make his radical or so-called functional Christology his own.

First, what relation is there between Schweitzer's ethic and that of Jesus? Are they the same?

Schweitzer admits that his ethic is essentially the Christian ethic. "The ethic of Reverence for Life," he says, "is the ethic of Love widened into universality. It is the ethic of Jesus, now recognized as a logical consequence of thought." [31] It is related, but it is also different. We discover it is the ethic of Jesus, first raised to a philosophical level of thought, second expanded into universal applicability, third infused with a more practical, continuing this-worldly orientation, and fourth made cosmic in scope.

As to the first, Schweitzer declares that "the raising of a dividing wall between philosophical ethics and religious ethics is based on the mistaken idea that the former are scientific and the latter non-scientific. But neither of them is either: they are both alike simply thought; only the one has freed itself from acceptance of the traditional religious world-view, while the other still maintains its connection with it." [32] One discipline works toward the basic principle of ethics "by a more intuitive process" and "like an artist who with the production of an important work of art opens up new horizons"; the other works "by a process which is more analytical." [33] But "it is the depth, not the method of the thought, which decides the matter." [34] "While religious moralists with one mighty word can get down to the waters flowing far below the surface, philosophical ethics often dig out nothing but a slight hollow in which a puddle forms." [35] "Nevertheless, it is *rational thinking alone* which is able to pursue the search for the basic principle with perseverance and hope of success." [36]

The ultimate features of the moral life, for Schweitzer, are still found in all their existential vigor simply stated in the life and teachings of Jesus, which no dry analytic philosophy could duplicate. But it cannot be accepted uncritically as it stands shored up only with religious enthusiasm, however sincere, or with theological embellishments, however reassuring. They have to be accredited by thought, indeed, made a necessary consequence of thought. What is meant by "necessity of thought," [37] a phrase that has unduly created a surfeit of criticism, should not be taken in any logicomathematical sense. It means that the nature of the situation or the case at hand which we regard constrains our reasoning to recognize its necessary implications. Or to state it more simply in the words of Heidegger, a necessity of thought is a "matter of compelling personal urgency." [38]

But can this be done? Can the ethical insights of Jesus be preserved by critical thought and made compelling apart from their Biblical matrix and theological framework? Schweitzer believed it was possible. Such an undertaking, he regretfully foresaw, would bring a painful disenchantment for many, but, at least he felt we could take heart in reason's faith that "every new truth means ultimately something won." [39]

Since for Schweitzer the essence of religion is not to be identified with any set of doctrinal statements or sacred tradition, but is simply the ardent search for truth coupled with a world- and life-Yea-Saying resulting in an active ethical devotion to life, the main criterion by which every religion is to be judged is "how far it produces permanent and profound incentives to the inward perfecting of personality and to ethical activity." [40] The Christian religion is to be revered only insofar as it embodies these principles. Indeed, all religions must be observed and tested in this way. If there comes forth from the research spent on the study of other religions anything in the way of universal principles that can serve the cause of man, they are

to be kept and treasured. "All religious truth must in the end
be capable of being grasped as something that stands to reason." [41]

Following the period of the Enlightenment, we are to understand that "the bonds between Christianity and active
thought were loosened, and the situation today is that Christianity has completely withdrawn into itself, and is concerned
only with the propagation of its own ideas, as such. It no longer
sees any use in proving them to be in agreement with thought,
but prefers that they be regarded as something altogether outside it, and occupying a superior position. It loses, however,
thereby its connection with the spiritual life of the time and
the possibility of exercising any real influence upon it." [42]

The Christian ethic, then, according to Schweitzer, must be
brought into a fearless relation to critical thought and established, not upon any kind of double standard of truth or supernatural revelation, but logically upon fact as far as possible and
upon deep reflection born of experience. In this way the ethic
of Jesus is taken out of its narrow apocalyptic and apologetic
context, rid of Biblical terminology, and put into more meaningful and cogent terms so that it may more readily be ap-
pealed to by all thinking people regardless of background or
belief. This rational grounding gives Schweitzer's ethic—and
Jesus'—its universal applicability.

Schweitzer also sees the necessity of translating the interim ethic of Jesus to fit the continuing movement of society
and history. Since Jesus was under the complete sway of the
expectation of the "supernatural and super-ethical Kingdom of
God," which led to a depreciation of the existing transient and
imperfect world in comparison with the eternal and perfect
world to come, his "ethics are concerned only with the attainment of inner perfection," not the "establishment of better
conditions in the world." [43] "This means that ethics are delivered from any need to listen to considerations of prudence,
which always means giving way to compromise and accepting
the will to the merely religiously good." [44] Jesus' ethics "do not

concern themselves with such a question as whether following out the command not to resist evil may not threaten the existence of religiously well-ordered social conditions." [45]

Schweitzer praises Jesus for compelling us "to look away from what we aim at and achieve in our moral activity" in order "to call ourselves to account for what we really are." But even though "we must never let our wrestling with the demands of absolute personal ethics slacken into contentment with the modest requirements of the relative and general," "no system of ethics can be complete until it calls upon men at one and the same time both for the achieving of inward perfection and for activity." [46]

Another way in which Schweitzer's ethic differs from the ethic of Jesus arises out of a question which personally plagued Schweitzer since his childhood. This concerns both philosophical as well as religious ethics. Can we discover, he asks, an ethic that will rid itself of the gross inconsistency of arbitrarily drawing the circle of ethics around human beings and excluding the rest of sentient creation of which man is only a small part? This was possible, he found, with his ethic of Reverence for Life. Schweitzer was forced to expand the ethic of Jesus beyond the confines of its purely human setting to include all life as the object of moral responsibility. This is what he terms the "universalization of altruism." Ethics must not stop short with human life alone. "The great fault of all ethics hitherto has been that they believed themselves to have to deal only with the relations of man to man." [47] Man is ethical "only when life as such is sacred to him, that of plants and animals as that of his fellow man, and when he devotes himself helpfully to all life that is in need of help. Only the universal ethic of the feeling of responsibility is an ever-widening sphere for all that lives"—is truly ethical. [48]

In an ecologically aware age, such as ours, these words are more pertinent and profound than when they were first written. Now Schweitzer's ethic no longer seems so foolish. To have reverence for animals, insects, and even plants is an obligation forced upon us against our wills. That a biological balance is necessary and must be maintained takes on the form of an ethical obligation. Because we did not extend the sphere of our ethical duties, in the past, to include *all* life, because we in callousness and wanton disregard, did not feel the moral compulsion to maintain and enhance all life, we are suddenly reaping the polluted fruits of our sins and neglect. As we wastefully kill other living things, we kill ourselves, for all Life is One. Now reverence for life truly becomes for our times a "necessity of thought."

Thus we perceive that Schweitzer's ethic is essentially the Christian ethic, but how different it actually is must be realized.

He does not measure his ethic by that of Jesus, but vice versa; he judges the Christian ethic by the principle of reasoned reflection and the epiphany of Reverence for Life, retaining and expanding what symbolizes the absolute ethic of love and leaving aside what is unessential. Or to put it more accurately, in the *spirit of Jesus,* Schweitzer worked toward the founding of that spirit in an ethical theory, rationally conceived as a necessity of thought, which would be universally applicable and cosmic in scope. Hence his philosophical orientation, his religious agnosticism, his radical rejection of traditional Christianity, and his extending the bounds of moral obligation to include all life whatsoever set his ethic apart from that of Jesus.

A second way in which Schweitzer's Radical theology qualifies the role and significance of Jesus is his acceptance of him only as the "Lord of our wills" and his rejection of him as the "Lord of our minds." "In reality, He is an authority for us," declares Schweitzer, "not in the sphere of knowledge but only in the realm of the will." [49] This personal appropriation by Schweitzer of the spiritualized Jesus who becomes the personification of his absolute ethic of love, and the rejection of him as the historically and metaphysically unique infallible Christ, has caused considerable confusion and consternation. It is the reason so many, such as Professor Rolff on one extreme,

believe that Schweitzer presents " 'a purely philosophical
ethic' " which " 'does not stand under the domination of religion at all,' " [50] and such writers as Clark on the other who
believe that Schweitzer is under the full religious sway of
"Jesus as the Christ" and that his ethical mysticism in reality
is a "Christ mysticism." [51] Though I find both are in error, I
fully sympathize with them, for the possibilities for both interpretations appear in Schweitzer. It again reinforces my
contention that Schweitzer can mean several things to many
people, for he speaks as a philosopher to the philosophers and
as a theologian to the theologians and it is not always easy to
know which umbrella to run under when the showers of critical analysis begin.

My thesis, as I have stated, is that both are held in one hand
in the form of a radical theology—which is no easy trick, if one
has ever tried it! Indeed, one runs the risk of becoming more
drenched by criticism than ever. But I take heart in the fact
that the rain falls on the justified as well as the unjustified, and
in this case I find Schweitzer fully justified in what he attempts
to achieve. It may not be an apt metaphor, but it is in keeping
with Hamilton's characterization of doing theology which "is
always like having six storm windows to cover eight windows." [52]

I agree with critics such as Rolff that Schweitzer's radical
theology is built upon the assumptions of his ethical philosophy and not upon the Christian message, but I also agree with
Clark and those of like mind that he speaks out of an intimate
religious attachment to Jesus as the Lord of his life which en-
livens his ethic of Reverence for Life. Elemental reason and
philosophy are the tonic and dominant notes on the Schweitzerian scale, Jesus is the third which unites the sounds into a
living chord. Schweitzer admits that in his thinking, " 'The
holy music of religion sounds softly but clearly!' " [53] The key
word here is "softly," which Clark apparently overlooked.
The spiritual Jesus is a strong but subtle influence in his life,
like the altos in a Bach chorale, not the brass in a Wagnerian
overture. "Mysticism," warns Schweitzer, "must never be

thought to exist for its own sake. It is not a flower, but only the calyx of a flower. Ethics are the flower." [54] If mysticism were the *dominant* factor in Schweitzer's thought, then it would be legitimate to hold he has a "Christ mysticism," which Clark does. But it is "only the calyx." It is ethics which is "the flower," and the ethics of Jesus were found wanting by Schweitzer and had to be expanded by thought. As I have already said, his thought should be described not as "ethical *mysticism*," but as "*ethical* mysticism."

Psychologically the motivation link of Schweitzer with Jesus is a curious trait in his personality. It is curious because his personal identity with Jesus, which has at times an almost childlike simplicity to it, is not derived from any theological or philosophical persuasion, and lies apart from the traditional interpretations. Most people cannot emotionally comprehend how a man can speak of Jesus in such devout and mystical terms without believing that Jesus is everything organized Christianity says he is, or at least cosmically unique in some way or other. Apparently we must again distinguish, as we similarly did in regard to his belief in God, between the scholarly imagination at work as it enters critically into the Biblical texts in order to mine their riches for Christian under-standing, fully utilizing the religious idioms and symbols for clarification, and the scholar's personal religious and philo-sophical interpretation of the same passages and ideas for his own life and times; or we may say the difference between his work as a Biblical scholar, his own intellectual beliefs, and the archetypal symbol enlivening those beliefs as well as his own personal life. It is true that they all interpenetrate; and more than any other contemporary world figure, it is true that Schweitzer's thought and life coalesce so completely that one cannot hope adequately to understand one without the other, but for the sake of accuracy they should be distinguished.

It is clear that the personality of Jesus made a tremendous im-pression on the mind of the boy [Schweitzer] from his earliest child-hood; this impression was by no means lessened when in later years his critical mind created a Jesus who is . . . very different to the traditional figure. The persuasive, uplifting and emancipating, power of a human . . . example is strikingly apparent in Schweitzer. For this to be possible, however, a special type of soul is needful, one whose will reacts with exceptional intensity to feelings of compassion and one moreover which is unusually alive to the impression which the personality of Jesus evokes; in short, a character capable of translating these emotions into actions.[55]

It is understandable why Schweitzer can write: " 'Jesus has simply taken me prisoner since my childhood. . . . My going to Africa was an act of obedience to Jesus.' " [56] Of course! What could be more understandable, more natural. Schweitzer intuitively identified himself with the figure of Jesus, as frequently happens when a sensitive person is grasped by the ideas and spirit of a charismatic individual, and Jesus became the symbolic focus of his unceasing moral energy. Jesus began "a mighty movement of ideas" which continued to flow through Schweitzer's remarkable life until the day he died still laboring as a "man for others" as the Master of his ethical life commanded him.

To take the personal remarks of Schweitzer such as the one above, and to glean the many orthodox-sounding statements Schweitzer makes in and around the fringes of the *Quest* or the *Mysticism of Paul* or his sermons, when he is addressing a strictly Christian audience in the familiar history-conditioned terminology, in order to weave them into an airtight justification that his ethical philosophy is taken prisoner by a Christ mysticism is misleading, and I caution against it. Such a conciliatory approach fails to take seriously the above distinctions.

I recognize that no single-shot solution will solve the matter, not even my own, for it is doubly difficult to understand any great personality where ordinary labels do not apply. The mark of genius is always complexity; and no person escapes contradiction, particularly the multi-sided Schweitzer. What adds to the difficulty of understanding him precisely is not only his social marginality but the fact that Schweitzer took his stand in an intensity of awareness that is isolated from ordinary solutions and common aims of twentieth-century man.

But despite the difficulties, I believe that a more accurate designation for the place of Jesus in Schweitzer's theology than the one Clark and others ascribe ought to be found.

My own opinion is that Schweitzer has a *Jesus* mysticism, not a *Christ* mysticism, and by that I mean it is an ethical, not a metaphysical or dialectical, mysticism. It is one that points us directly and concretely to the world, to a this-worldly happening, to a freeing power in our midst, to a man beside other men, for Jesus is not a divine entity to contemplate or worship, but a living will to obey. This places Schweitzer closer to Hamilton, Cox, van Buren, and Novak, than to Altizer and Vahanian.[57] I shy from the term "Christ" and refuse to spend time laboring over another reinterpretation, qualifying it in order to make it mean what I mean by a Jesus mysticism because it has too many cloying connotations. I agree with Novak, we ought to try to do without it. It has become so overlaid with theological and dialectical encrustations that it sinks the religious imagination back into the same unwelcomed conceptual ruts. Though it is an unwieldy phrase, a Jesus mysticism has fewer theological ghosts to combat.

To state it as simply as possible, Jesus is "the supreme spiritual and religious authority" [58] for Schweitzer because he finds the heart of the universal ethic of love resounding forcibly in him. The Universal Will-to-cosmic-and-human-relatedness, which undulates mysteriously within us all, was greatly amplified in Jesus' life because, among other things, the interim atmosphere of the eschatological expectation of the coming Jewish Kingdom of Justice and Peace tuned it up to its highest pitch. In Jesus we suddenly and briefly catch a glimpse of the law of love in its absolute form. And the vision that all lives are united directly in the power of a selfless love, negating the alienating effects of a fallen world, miraculously was not gained at the expense of world- and life-affirmation. There is a world-passing-away rejection in Jesus, but it exists, inconsistently, within a strong affirmation of the world and of life. For these reasons Jesus becomes for Schweitzer the ideal exemplification of the necessary elements that man's spiritual life requires for the attainment of its fullest expression.

To accept Jesus as the living example of the good life, or of love, or of the fullest expression of man's humanity, and to feel the power of his spirit still at work in the world do not necessarily entail belief that he was God, or the Son of God, or the Logos, or the supernatural Christ, or some metaphysical dialectic channel into which God poured himself once-upon-a-time into the world. "Schweitzer will have nothing to do with these abstract metaphysical problems. For Schweitzer the personality of Christ is no theological conundrum. Our knowledge of Him does not depend on dialectical subtleties. It comes to us directly as the impact of Life upon life. His spirit is alive and at work in the world today, and we can know Him, not by mystifying ourselves with speculations about His Person and His Nature, but by entering into the fellowship of His sufferings, by doing His will, by obedience to His absolute ethic of love." [59]

Schweitzer does not try to create a mysterious theological enigma out of the man Jesus for devotional purposes or for the sake of making him unique. Christianity has gambled everything on this and almost lost everything. This is now a dead end; Schweitzer knows that Jesus is not unique as a historical individual; he is not unique in any metaphysical sense; he is not unique in his having lived, loved, suffered, and died—for many men, great men, have done the same. He is not the only man who has revealed the Sacred to us. He is not the most creative, the most erudite, the most intelligent man who ever lived. He is not even unique in what he preached, since his parables can be duplicated in Jewish Wisdom literature. His ethical insights are not complete, for even Schweitzer has revealed to us a broader commandment of love.

Then why? Why Jesus?

To put it very bluntly, *Jesus* is not unique. "They all were looking for a King . . . to lift them high; Thou camest a little baby thing, that made a woman cry." [60] We have been looking for something deep, complex, and utterly mysterious, when in reality it is something unesoterically simple and present already in our hearts. It is the power of life touching life that still flows from him to us that is unique. It is what men have done and are still willing to do in his name that is unique. It is *because* he was human and fallible, and still accomplished what he did, that grips our humanity. "Jesus is the one to whom I repair, the one before whom I stand, the one whose way with others is also to be my way," writes Hamilton, "because there is something there, in his words, his life, his way with others, his death, that I do not find elsewhere." [61] If it is uniqueness that it required, it is found in these ways. It is because we desire and need a Christ, in the first place; because we desire to spiritualize Jesus and the events surrounding him, *and can,* that makes it all unique. It is not *Jesus* that is unique but the fact that he makes *us* unique!

Reverence for Life may be a compelling necessity of thought for Schweitzer, but a Jesus or Christ mysticism is not. Does, or can, Schweitzer command that *this* also be a universal experience for all people? Do we have to be "prisoners of Christ" before we have reverence for life? No. I abjure this interpretation of Schweitzer. Jesus is *not* the *only* embodiment of God or the Will-to-Love. We do not discover or enhance our wills-to-human-concern exclusively by way of Jesus or a Christ mysticism. For *Christians,* yes; their ethical wills may be so enhanced; but Schweitzer's ethic is an ethic that goes beyond that of Jesus and is universalized for all men. This is what he means by the spiritualized Jesus concept. Jesus is *the* example for Schweitzer *personally,* and for Christians, as to how to perfect the spirit. But for others this need not necessarily be the case. They may feel the leadings of the Spirit of reverence for life in other ways whether they identify its supreme example with Jesus or not. Schweitzer himself universalized or spiritualized Jesus with this in mind. As even Clark himself admits,

Schweitzer "uses the spiritual Jesus as the source of inspiration for those very ideals which the historical Jesus could not serve as authority." [62] And Schweitzer writes: "It was not Jesus Himself who gave its perfect spiritual form to the truth which He brought into the world. . . . It received this in the course of the working of His spirit in subsequent history." [63]

A distinction must be made therefore between Schweitzer's ethic of Reverence for Life, his universal appeal to all men, which is an enlargement of the ethic of Jesus, and his own personal appropriation of Jesus as Lord of our wills. The latter is not as essential to his New Religion as the attaching of a Christ mysticism to him would imply.[64]

In the last analysis it is Schweitzer himself who expresses the role and significance of Jesus in his thought more eloquently and clearly than anyone:

Our relationship to the historical Jesus must be simultaneously truthful and free. We give history its due and then make ourselves free from its conceptual materials. But we bow before the mighty will that stands behind it, and we seek to serve this will in our time, that it may be born in us in new vitality and fruitfulness, and that it may work toward fulfillment in us and in the world.

But it is not true to say that we possess the idea of the moral perfection of the world and the ideas we have of what must be done in our time because we have obtained them through historical revelation. *These ideas lie within us; they are given with the ethical will.* Because Jesus, as one Who stood in the line of succession of the greatest among the prophets, summed up these ideas and taught them with the utmost thoroughness and directness, and because He embodied them in His own great personality, He helps us to be similarly dedicated and to become ethical forces in our own time.

This interpretation of religion and of the person Jesus is usually dismissed as one-sidedly moralistic and rationalistic. In order to overcome this reaction, we need only call to mind the fact that if this interpretation is really alive and potent, it encompasses religion in its totality. For all that man can really say about salvation boils down to this: it means being set free from the world and from ourselves through a fellowship of the will with Jesus, and being filled with power and peace and courage for life. Let no one forget that Jesus Himself was essentially a rationalist and a moralist. That He was conditioned by late-Jewish metaphysics is incidental.

In the final analysis, our relationship to Jesus is of a mystical sort. No personality of the past can be transported to the present by means of historical reflection or affirmations about His authoritative significance. We enter into relationship with Him only by being brought together in the recognition of a common will, and by experiencing a clarification, enrichment, and quickening of our will through His. Thus do we find ourselves again in Him. *In this sense every deeper relationship between men partakes of a mystical quality. So our religion, in so far as it is to be regarded as specifically Christian, is not so much a "Jesus-cult" as it is a Jesus-mysticism.*[65]

It is plain that Schweitzer does not cling to any historical incarnational models. There is nothing of the atonement theory in his regard of Jesus' life and death. Nor does his ethical interpretation conceal a hidden process of redemption or supernatural transformation. Participation in the "enrichment and quickening" of our lives through His will mediates an encounter with the deepest currents of our humanity or will-to-live and places us more engagingly in the life of the world beside other men as brothers. Jesus is freed for us from magic, myth, and miracle by Schweitzer, and by so doing he frees us also and frees Jesus *for* us. Jesus can now be fully faced in his rightful place among us. Perhaps for the first time he comes into a nontheological perspective, and our reasons for following him become tractable, testable, tryable, and full of risk—the inevitable ingredient of every human decision. Just because there is no guarantee, we are called upon to show forth the rationality of our decision in every future action. Now he resides in the real, competitive arena of all men, all religions, and all ultimate expressions, and his ideals now are forced to come alive in us, or be pushed aside.

Schweitzer is convinced that despite the risk of every hu-

man encounter, once one comes into contact with the spirit
of Jesus, he will be grasped by something elemental and inexorable that will never let him go. Something that is real as
rock and right as rain. Who is Jesus? What is he? Why can he
be regarded as the Lord of our lives, even for those who have
no religion? Neither historical evidence, nor philosophical
proof, nor theological faith can in the last analysis answer for
us, Schweitzer realizes. He can only allow each one to discover for himself what it means. He only replies: Obey his
commands, try his way, catch his spirit of creative concern,
"And to those who obey Him, whether they be wise or simple,
He will reveal Himself in the toils, the conflicts, the sufferings
which they shall pass through in His fellowship, and, as an
ineffable mystery, they shall learn in their own experience,
Who He is." [66]

I wonder whether with this interpretation it could be said
that Schweitzer is more radical, in some instances, than the
Radical theologians? I have always felt that the more important
question facing the Radicals was not how can we live the
religious life without God, but how can we live as Christians
in a time of the death of Christ? I am convinced that the crisis
of the death of God was one of the results, not the cause, of the
current ferment, that it came after the crisis of the death of
Christ which most Christian theologians were unwilling to
admit.[67] It was the *Christ* also who "died the death of a thousand qualifications" and question-begging tactics, not just God.
But since the Christian doctrine of God was irrevocably
bound to a soteriological doctrine of Christ, the inevitable occurred. I often feel that the Radicals got rid of the Father in
order to save the Son, and that they are attending the wrong
funeral service. My contention is that they should not attend
either service, seeking the living among the dead.

In all their worry and anguish over the fact that the symbol
"God" is broken or meaningless, or that it is devoid of power
for our modern faith because it is so culture-bound, so rela-
tivistically stamped with past questions and answers, the Radi-

cals inconsistently have forgotten that the one tenet to which they repair, Jesus as the Christ, is also just as time-bound as Schweitzer made clear. If the word, and belief in, "God" is so culture-bound, then so is the word and belief in "Christ," so is "the Christian way of life," "Christian ethics," and "Christian concern." If the Biblical "God" is dead because of a past-world relation, so is "Jesus Christ." By the same token, if we can meaningfully renew, as Hamilton, for instance, importunes, the ideals of faith, love, cross, resurrection, kerygma, eschatology, etc., so can we just as well, or just as poorly, as the case may be, renew the term and meaning of "God." *All* these theological concepts have been made into idolatrous absolutes, or have disintegrated by analysis, or have been made effete by new knowledge, not just "God."

I do not think a new round of Christological excursions, especially in the absence of any profound ontology, is the best attack upon our present problems. Altizer, for example, admonishes us in his "wager" to remove God and free Christ, because he believes a transcendent God stands in the way to a full epiphany of the living Christ.[68] But I wonder if the reverse might not be as essential? We might confront ourselves with the larger summons: "Remove Christ and free God!" or at least free Jesus for men as Schweitzer has done. The tyranny of the Christocentric predicament unfortunately still holds the Christian theologian captive, including some of the Radicals; and this may be the very thing that is blocking future forms of effective belief.

Carl Braaten reflects this in his comment that "the burning question in theology today is no longer about the shape of Christology but about the future shape of humanity. . . . Christology will have to be reconceived as eschatological interpretation of the history of each individual, of collective mankind, and of the cosmic environment. For I doubt that very soon there will be many left, not even in our seminaries, who will care a fig about 'the shape of Christology.' " [69]

Perhaps a more radical challenge to Christian thought is still in the offing. Perhaps we will have to learn to live as Christians not only without God, but also without Christ. And it might be important then to be able to turn to such pioneers as Schweitzer, who have moved into this frontier and hewn out for us, if not a mighty fortress, at least a place to stand as men beside others.

VI

The Phenomenology of Hope

A FULL REPORT of Schweitzer's radical theology of Reverence for Life is incomplete without inclusion of his interpretation of the significance of the concept of the Kingdom of God, and the interesting relationship in which it stands to the recent revival of the importance of eschatology in the various theories comprising what is called today the Theology of Hope. "Although it has usually been the poor step-sister in the household of theology, eschatology, the study of Christian hope, is today once again claiming a central place. Theologians such as Jürgen Moltmann and Johannes Metz are working today with the assumption that Albert Schweitzer was right when he saw Christianity as essentially eschatological. They see the need not just to recover eschatology, but to rethink the whole theological tradition from the perspective of hope."[1] The central mystery of Christianity for Schweitzer is not, and was not originally, the problem of salvation or redemption, or faith in the resurrection and forgiveness of sins; it is the secret of the Kingdom of God and the hope of its miraculous transformation of the world and life in a New Creation. "To be a Christian means to be possessed and dominated by a hope of the Kingdom of God, and a will to work for it," writes Schweitzer.[2] "Until this comes about Christianity will stand before the world like a wood in the barrenness of winter."[3]

From its earliest inception as the Day of the Lord, a time of justice and peace to which the Old Testament prophets

looked forward, to the belief in the rise of a conquering political warrior of the house of David, to the postexilic hope in a
supernatural vicegerent of Jehovah who would restore Israel's
covenanted place as the chosen people, to the suffering-servant
concept of the Messiah of Second Isaiah, the idea of the Kingdom of God has passed through successive prisms of interpretation, each reflecting the particular social, political, and religious needs of its age. By the first century there arose, by
reason of further changes in the world situation, a more virulent apocalyptic form of Jewish eschatology which prophesied
the sudden and very soon appearance of the end of the age,
the coming of the Messiah, the Last Judgment, and the violent
but miraculous transformation of the world of God in which he
would be all in all. It was into this turbulent and expectant atmosphere that Jesus entered upon the stage of history.

Schweitzer's interpretation of Jesus and the early church
as dominated by this late Jewish eschatological belief stirred
up a storm of controversy which has raged back and forth ever
since it was first made public in 1906. Orthodox and liberal
alike were incensed that Schweitzer had the audacity to interpret Jesus in the light of a first-century apocalypticism and
drag them both alive and shrieking into the twentieth century
in the name of historical truth. It jarred their sophisticated
religious sensitivities, and they balked at the thought. Yet, almost sixty years later after the apocalyptic dust had settled,
Schweitzer's Jesus was still ominously standing as the im-
perious proclaimer of the coming Kingdom for his age in which
he was rooted and as a stranger to ours forever.

The primitive Christian hope of the immediate coming of
God's Kingdom was based on the teaching of Jesus who regarded himself as the suffering servant who was to be instrumental in ushering in the New Age. Yet while Jesus was fully
caught up in the apocalyptic vision of his time, Schweitzer
finds that the ethical, spiritual demands of the Kingdom were
of equal if not greater importance in his life and teachings.
This was his unique contribution. "Jesus spiritualizes the con-

cept of the Kingdom of God, in that he brings it into subjection to his ideal and ethic of love. In due time this transforms the conception of the Kingdom." [4] But before this subtle transformation began to work in the minds of Paul and the members of the early church, the effect of the nonfulfillment of Jesus' prophecy and the disappointment that the Kingdom did not appear at the time of his death had to be grappled with. The important factor for Christianity was not that Jesus was wrong, which was shattering enough to those early believers, and now to us, but that there occurred a transformation of the faith which enabled it to survive the surrender of the original expectation. This was mainly due to the religious genius of Paul, who was able to maintain the fervor of the expectancy of the New Age by believing it was still to come, and at the same time believing that by Jesus' self-sacrifice it was already manifested. "Through mystical fellowship with the crucified and risen Jesus Christ, believers already share with him the supernatural quality of life in the Kingdom." [5] Paul saw it as something postponed for a short time, and yet as a power that could be participated in in the meantime.

Paul's doctrine of a brief postponement was by necessity gradually abandoned, until the Kingdom hoped for some time became the "one far-off divine event" toward which all history moves in its final culmination. The original enthusiastic expectation of Jesus and Paul, like a dreamy mountain mist, evaporated before the continuing blaze of history. The passing of this hope brought an elaborate reshaping of faith and momentous changes in doctrine. Following generations were to give their particular interpretation of the Kingdom of God until it became, not the central motivating faith, but one doctrine among many. Other beliefs eventually usurped its place. Attention was concentrated now upon the nature of Christ, the efficacy of the Eucharist, the forgiveness of sins, the redemptive role of the church, and eternal life. Little by little the hope gave way to "correct belief" (*orthodoxos*), and the Kingdom of God was identified with the church itself and its promise of a heavenly afterlife which it alone could guarantee.

Though the primitive form of Jesus' expectation is incredible to us today and has to be abandoned, Schweitzer insists that we must return to the original enthusiasm and spiritual outlook which Jesus' eschatological hope contains for us. We must rethink for our age the significance which the Kingdom of God and the eschatological ideas in the Bible have for our existence. Both Jesus' and Paul's beliefs were "magnificent structures," according to Schweitzer, which despite their pre-scientific grounding, can "provide material which could be used for buildings of another style." [6] That this is so was made possible for us by Paul himself, whom we have to thank for preserving the vigor and importance of the future hope of the Kingdom, for he freed it "from its temporal limitations" and made it "valid for all time." [7]

> Men feared that to admit the claims of eschatology would abolish the significance of His [Jesus'] words for our time; and hence there was a feverish eagerness to discover in them any elements that might be considered not eschatologically conditioned. . . .
>
> But in reality that which is eternal in the words of Jesus is *due to the very fact that they are based on an eschatological worldview,* and contain the expression of a mind for which the contemporary world with its historical and social circumstances no longer had any existence. They are appropriate, therefore, to any world, for in every world they raise the man who dares to meet their challenge . . . above his world and his time, making him inwardly free, so that he is fitted to be, in his own world and in his own time, a simple channel of the power of Jesus.[8]

Exactly what is it in the New Testament eschatology that is "eternal" and "valid for all time" to which Schweitzer encourages us to return? Can a demythologized eschatology be of any use to us today? Can we preserve the hope, which emanates from Jesus and Paul, apart from its apocalyptic framework?

As Schweitzer spiritualizes the life and teachings of Jesus, and universalizes his ethic, so he does the same with the concept of the Kingdom of God. This he feels is wholly justified since it was Jesus himself who began this spiritual deepening of humanistic ideals, and it was Paul who continued it. Jesus "spiritualized" the conception of the Jewish apocalyptic Kingdom in that he brought it "into subjection to his ideal and ethic of love," and it was Paul who recognized that the essence of the Kingdom consisted "in the rule of the Spirit." [9] The way in which it will be brought about for Paul "is by the coming of Jesus Christ to rule in our hearts and through us in the whole world. In the thought of Paul the supernatural Kingdom is beginning to become the ethical and with this to change from the Kingdom to be expected into something which has to be realized." [10] In this way the freeing of Christian eschatology from its particularistic and historical strictures, and the preservation of some of its invaluable insights for all ages, began. "It is for us to take the road," says Schweitzer, "which this prospect opens up." [11] We must pass from *expectation* of the Kingdom to *experience* of it. We must move from its cultic to its universal implications. We must divest it of its apocalyptic imagery, its temporal and spatial literalism, and its dogmatism, and direct its ethical fervor of transforming love and hope toward the realities of this world. "Only as it comes to be understood as something ethical and spiritual, rather than supernatural, . . . can the Kingdom of God regain, in our faith, the force that it had for Jesus and the early Church. Christianity must have a firm hold of this, if it is to remain true to itself," [12] for it is "only through the idea of the kingdom of God that religion enters into relationship with civilization." [13]

If this interpretation of the Kingdom sounds similar to those of Protestant liberalism, such as the social gospel of Rauschenbusch, which appeared in the early part of the twentieth century, the obvious answer is, it *is* similar. Schweitzer did not reject liberalism's ethical account of Jesus; he rejected its misuse of historical fact. The liberals were historically wrong, but religiously right. They were wrong to believe Jesus was a

modern social reformer who viewed the coming of the Kingdom as realized by a long-range, cooperative effort between
man and God. They were correct in interpreting it as an ethical challenge to make the dream of lasting justice and peace
on earth a reality by living according to his utter devotion to
God and man. This is the reason he sounds so inconsistent at
times saying, "We must take the ethical religion of Jesus out
of the setting of his world-view and put it in our own" on one
hand,[14] and "It is not given to *history* to disengage that which
is abiding and eternal in the being of Jesus from the historical
forms in which it worked itself out, and to introduce it into
our world as a living influence," [15] on the other. But we must
remember the Schweitzerian axiom that "the abiding and
eternal in Jesus is absolutely independent of *historical* knowledge and can only be understood by contact with His spirit
which is still at work in the world." [16]

The vision which Jesus released into the world is something invaluable. It makes little difference in what crude vessel
of thought it originally appeared. Theology only recently has
been able to separate the two. In the past it often came to
grief because it insisted upon basing its beliefs concerning
certain historical events upon value interpretations of these
events. An evaluational interpretation may of itself be revealing and may lead to further insights into many religious aspects of nature, man, and God. But this does *not* prove that
the events which are being interpreted are therefore historically true. The reverse holds equally well. This is Schweitzer's
point. He is not so much inconsistent on this point, as ignored
or misunderstood.

It appears, from what was said above, that Kant's and
Ritschl's influence upon Schweitzer's ethical interpretation of
the Kingdom of God is as strong as it is upon his view of Jesus.
All religious statements seem to be reduced to ethical ones;
and religious symbols to inspirational aids to moral commitment. I tried to show, with some success, I hope, that Schweitzer's radical theology involves more than this; it also possesses

a cosmic dimension. I believe this can be seen in regard to his concept of eschatology as being central to our religious world view.

Jürgen Moltmann, in his *The Theology of Hope*, refers to Schweitzer's rediscovery of eschatology for our age as "undoubtedly one of the most important events in recent Protestant theology." [17] But he goes on to state that Schweitzer "had no eschatological sense at all. . . . The consequences which he drew from his discovery of the apocalyptic of Jesus were aimed at the final conquest and annihilation of what he considered an illusionary eschatologism." [18] It may be true that Schweitzer is more attuned to the presence of "eternal truth" in Jesus' thought than to the eschatological character of Biblical thought per se, but there are statements in Schweitzer which show that he had a more sympathetic grasp of the significance of eschatological thought than Moltmann believes, particularly if we translate Biblical eschatology, as Moltmann has done, into a phenomenology of hope.

To substantiate this, I begin with a quote from Schweitzer's *Quest* which I consider to be a key passage in understanding his concept of the Kingdom of God:

The Messianic secret of Jesus is the basis of Christianity, since it involves the de-nationalising and the spiritualisation of Jewish eschatology. . . .

It is the primal fact, the starting-point of a process which manifests itself, indeed, in Christianity, but cannot fully work itself out even here, of a movement in the direction of inwardness which brings all religious magnitudes into the one indivisible spiritual present, and which Christian dogmatic has not ventured to carry to its completion. The Messianic consciousness of the uniquely great Man of Nazareth sets up a struggle between the present and the beyond, and *introduces that resolute absorption of the beyond by the present,* which in looking back we recognise as the history of Christianity, and of which we are conscious in ourselves as the essence of religious progress and experience—a process of which the end is not yet in sight.[19]

Professor William Beardslee, whom I have to thank for personally underscoring for me the significance of this passage, uses it in the introduction to his study of the "motif of fulfillment" in the Synoptic Gospels.[20] He writes, "To me this is one of the seminal passages in Schweitzer's book, since it moves far beyond the Ritschlianism which its reference to 'spiritualization,' for instance, suggests, to a kind of 'process' view of the absorption of the transcendent in the immanent, which shows how deeply prophetic Schweitzer was of so much that has happened in modern theology." [21]

Schweitzer does *not* take the apocalyptic or thoroughgoing eschatology of Jesus as his main point of departure for his reflections or methodological procedures, as does Wolfhart Pannenberg or Jürgen Moltmann, for example. But it is still, to use Pannenberg's words, a "thermal current" running through his considerations of the importance and uniqueness of Jesus' message for us today. The way in which its influence appears is subtle, and it is up to the reader to keep it so in order to see exactly in what ways Schweitzer anticipated the recent uses, and misuses, of it by the theologians of Hope.

Schweitzer takes Jesus not only as the prime exemplar of our ethical wills but also as the pioneer and first sign of the New Age, which is a religious way of expressing that hope for the future Kingdom of Peace that frees men from pain, oppression, and strife. This is not merely a faith expression for Schweitzer. Jesus literally points to the presence of some reality universally at work in the world, some "primal fact" of a process which makes us new creatures. To be a "prisoner of Christ" is for Schweitzer, as it was for Paul, to be a prisoner of the continuous transforming power of the Will-to-love, of the beyond made present in him.

A denial of the world coupled with the belief that the Kingdom of God is not present but comes only at the end of time banishes the effective presence of hope and condemns man "to refrain from all efforts to improve the present situation." [22] "Hopelessness," declares Schweitzer, "about the present situation goes along with belief in the Kingdom of God coming at the end of time," [23] i.e., with belief in a supernatural Kingdom whose reality is still beyond us in some absolute future, whose fullness is not yet a present force. Hope is in vain and powerless if the possibility of sharing "with one another the blessings of a new creation" [24] does not work mightily in our midst now. "Our hope of the Kingdom is directed to the essential and spiritual meaning of it, and we believe in that as a miracle wrought by the Spirit in making men obedient to the will of God. But we must cherish in our hearts this belief in the coming of the Kingdom through the miracle of the Spirit with the same ardour with which the primitive Christianity cherished its hope of the translation of the world into the supernatural condition." [25] With the coming of Jesus the seeds of the Future Kingdom were sown, and are continually sown, spiritually germinating the present with inspiration and the reality of the not-yet.

It is all too easy to believe that what religious value Jesus has for Schweitzer he has *in spite of* his eschatological world view when in point of fact Schweitzer states that it is actually *because* of it. This sounds strange, but it is not a plea that we keep his apocalypticism intact, or accept it; it is an awareness of the fantastic effects the literal belief in the end of the world and the coming reign of God had upon Jesus' whole orientation and way of thinking.

For example, the ethic of Jesus is transformed by his eschatological hope; it is thrown into its highest relief by the nearness of the divine light of God's Kingdom. The Jewish apocalyptic expectation is the fire in which Jesus refines his peoples' finest ethical expressions and burns away the dross of expediency, ambiguity, compromise, and legalistic emendations. The absolute ethic of love appears in all its purity and potency, not only in his teachings of the coming Kingdom, but also in his life which he identified with the will of God. Embodying the ideals of the spirit was not only made essential by him, but possible, now that God's power, the power of his Kingdom, was already at work among men, helping them to become perfect even as their Father in heaven is perfect. This is the reason Jesus could speak in such superlatives and judge with such absoluteness. His extreme ethical commands make sense, and do not become the product of the feverish brain of some utopian visionary, if seen in the light of the interim period of preparation between the passing away of the natural world and the coming of the new. Why count the cost now of earthly treasures? What gain will be had by worrying over the petty exigencies of daily life? Why not leave father and mother? brothers and sisters? Why not give away all one's goods to feed the poor? What is of more value than the one "pearl of great price"—participation in God's Kingdom of righteousness and love? It is this version of the Messianic hope, however wrong, we have to thank for revealing to us the heights to which men must go, and are capable of going, to gain favor in God's sight.

Also, by reason of his eschatological world view, Jesus' ethic contains the proper balance of world- and life-negation, which according to Schweitzer is an indispensable ingredient in a living ethic. For Jesus the old must pass away to make way for the new. This evil world would be done away with with the appearance of God's supernatural Kingdom. He rejected this life in order to affirm the life in the world to come. Yet unlike most religious visionaries, he did not pessimistically reject this world, regarding it as an illusion, in favor of an otherworldly escape. The original Sacred was not back in time, nor outside of time; it was found only in a movement through this world and time. Though it is inconsistent, Jesus held a world-negation side by side with a world-affirmation. His rejection of the evils of the world did not urge him toward asceticism or withdrawal from the world, but strangely enough more toward the world and into life. This is possible only if we realize with Paul that we must be *in* the world, but not *of* the world. We are not completely submerged into, or identified with, the world or whatever *is;* we are children of the *ought,* who have

become spiritually different from the world by being transformed by the creative love of him who is still to come.

"Christianity is not consistent," Schweitzer admits. "In the
bedrock of its pessimism there are optimistic veins, for it is
not only the religion of redemption but of the Kingdom of
God. Therefore it wishes and hopes for a transformation of
the world." [26] "Jesus . . . demands that we should become
free from the world, and at the same time that we should be
active in the world. . . . To be glad instruments of God's
love in this imperfect world is the service to which men are
called, and it forms a preparatory stage to the bliss that awaits
them in the perfected world, the Kingdom of God." [27] It is in
the "peculiar tension between pessimism and optimism" that
"the uniqueness of the religion of Jesus" lies, says Schweitzer.

After a concerted search for a religious world view which is
world- and life-affirming, or optimistic, it is puzzling to find
Schweitzer praising Jesus for including a world- and life-negation, or pessimism, in his ethics. Is Schweitzer also inconsistent
for speaking of the necessity of life-negation as an essential
part of a "deepened world- and life-affirmation"? How does this
element fit into his own ethic of Reverence for Life?

"In the ethical man natural happenings come into contradiction with themselves. Nature knows only a blind affirmation
of life. The will-to-live which animates natural forces and living beings is concerned to work itself out unhindered. But in
man this natural effort is in a state of tension with a mysterious effort of a different kind. Life-affirmation exerts itself to
take up life-negation into itself in order to serve other living
beings by self-devotion, and to protect them, even, it may be,
by self-sacrifice, from injury or destruction." [28] Through life-
negation we "abhor that which is evil," through life-affirmation
we "cleave to that which is good." In the world we find that
it is necessary to negate those things which retard and destroy
the proper fulfillment of the individual, whether it is cancer
or our own greediness, which, of course, are "natural." We
cannot become more moral by becoming more like the world.

There are events in the world, and aspects of ourselves, that are corrosive and destructive which must be negated and fought against. Following one's natural instincts does not necessarily lead to altruistic action. One cannot affirm all aspects of self, life, and the world indiscriminately and embrace them optimistically and remain ethical without gross reservations. "Nature within her inmost self divides/To trouble men with having to take sides." Life-negation, in this sense, must therefore become an element within our ethical affirmation of life. "On the foundation of world-affirmation, life-negation takes its place as a means of helping forward this affirmation of other life than its own. It is not life-denial in itself that is ethical, but only such as it stands in the service of world-affirmation and becomes purposive within it." [29]

The general bland affirmation of the world and of life today by Christianity not only weakens it as an ethical, but also as a spiritual, force. If it is to maintain its prophetic voice, its affirmation "must . . . be Christianized and transfigured by the personal rejection of the world which is preached in the sayings of Jesus." [30] Failure to do this will "unstring the bow" of Christianity and make it "a mere sociological instead of a religious force." [31] (Secular theologians please take note!)

The resignation of Jesus to things earthly, to painful and enigmatic events beyond man's control, is also stressed by Schweitzer as an important by-product of Jesus' eschatological viewpoint. It is a spiritual gift that Schweitzer freely and willingly accepts, not only for himself but, in the name of man, for men today who are moving not nearer but farther away from the strength and courage that such peace of soul, that passeth all understanding, brings. It is not a resignation that collapses all hope into inactive despair or withdraws from the world viewed as a meaningless round of events. It does not mean that we do not take the world seriously, the world still remains the very arena of man's opportunity and God's challenge. It is a healthy resignation that prevents the frenzies of fanatical activity or despondent acquiescence, which often attack us out of our frustration over not being able to know everything, control everything, and be everything, from overwhelming us. But there is a time when men must learn to let go and reserve their strength for being equal to those tasks which are closer at hand, for we are surrounded by an impenetrable mystery; our times are in its hands. The resignation of Jesus lies, not at the active periphery of his resolves for the Kingdom, but at the heart of his love for God. It simply means that at the center there is a stillness. "True resignation is not a becoming weary of the world, rather it is the quiet triumph . . . which the will-to-live celebrates at the hour of its greatest need over the circumstances of life. It flourishes only in the soil of deep world- and life-affirmation." [32] This is the reason it flourished so magnificently in Jesus; and it is why Schweitzer extols it as worthy of emulation. "The first spiritual act in man's experience is reverence for life. The consequences of it is that he comes to realize his dependence upon events quite beyond his control. Therefore he becomes resigned. And this is the second spiritual act: resignation." [33]

The importance of Jesus' eschatological orientation, and its influence on Schweitzer, can also be seen in his statements regarding the impotence of the past to rule over our lives or call religion into being. His belief, for instance, that we can only understand the spirit of Jesus as it meets us here and now, as new life for us in the present, and that what is abiding in him cannot be mediated for us by historical studies or something that occurred in a past event, brings to mind Moltmann's conviction that for Christianity the "God of history" must be changed into the "God of the future," as he was originally in Biblical eschatology,[34] for God meets us only out of the newness of the future. For Moltmann, the new is not something the church carries over from the past, but it is literally and constantly a new creation out of nothing.[35] For Schweitzer, Jesus is a living reality that meets us out of our hope for the future in partnership as spiritual co-creators of the New Age, or Kingdom of God. No occurrence nor memory from the past, however divine or precious, has the power per se to accomplish such a transformation for us, or with us, in the present. "History," declares Schweitzer, "can destroy the present; it can reconcile the present with the past; can even to a certain extent transport the present into the past; but to contribute to the making of the present is not given unto it." [36] The Gospel of Jesus, "which is wholly orientated to the Kingdom of God," [37] is alive for us today because he did not look back to a time to be regained, or an Eden to be restored, but forward into the world to the newness of the Kingdom. The eternal perspective which Jesus released into the world cannot be gained by a repetition of past beliefs and acts. It is the eternally new. This view of the future, this opening up for all men of all times the possibility of the continuous renewal by the spirit, of being made a new person and of transforming the world, which Schweitzer discovers in Jesus, makes Schweitzer's words so intriguingly prophetic of recent trends and emphases in the Theology of Hope today.

It seems obvious to me that the eschatological outlook of Jesus and his early followers which Schweitzer discovers in the New Testament is not regarded by him as something incidental to the Christian faith which he dismissed without serious theological consideration. Its implications still have valuable import for us, according to him. Hence, I disagree that he has "no eschatological sense at all."

"Without its intense eschatological hope," writes Schweitzer, "the Gospel would have perished from the earth, crushed by the weight of historic catastrophes. But, as it was, by the mighty power of evoking faith which lay in it, eschatology made good in the darkest times Jesus' sayings about the imperishability of His words." [38]

If Schweitzer could praise Paul because he was "the champion of all thinkers who . . . have the courage to translate the thought-forms of primitive Christian belief into those which are proper to the world-view of their own times," [39] then he would applaud the work of Ernst Bloch, Johannes ·

Metz, Jürgen Moltmann, and Wolfhart Pannenberg, who have reclaimed the significance of the Kingdom of God concept and have grafted their new reinterpretations of history, society, God, man, and redemption onto the stock root of Christian eschatology. Whether he would find them "proper" or not, I suppose, is beside the point. The concept, however, at the hands of these men, has come under a far more subtle and far-reaching analysis and interpretation than ever before. Indeed, the original meaning and thrust of the idea is, at times, almost unrecognizable. The literal apocalyptic anticipation of the end of the age we meet in Jesus, and the early community is made to jump through an assortment of hermeneutic hoops with fascinating heuristic agility. It is demythologized, psychologized, ontologized, socialized, cosmicized, epistemologized, Marxistized, and Dionysianized. Eschatology is definitely "in." Christian theologians have moved (again) from the suburbs of Athens to the inner city of Jerusalem. It is the new name today of the continuing phenomenological study of religion, and reinterpretation of Biblical concepts. In a way, it is also another nod of recognition by theology toward process philosophy, which I find promising, and toward the continuing dialogue with the bases of Marxist faith, which I find imperative. Newness, prophecy, change, futurity, vision, hope: these are the key terms in this exciting trend which tries to avoid "the pessimism which people saw in neo-orthodoxy" or "the optimism . . . in its successor, secular theology." [40] Its motto is: "Where there's hope, there's life."

The theologians of Hope are not concerned with the historical problems of Biblical eschatology, they are not trying to reactivate a primitive millennialist cult enthusiasm, they are interested in the secular translation of eschatology as hope for the future. The crucial question, as they see it, is: What use, if any, is the generative force of this powerful belief for our time? Can such a radical hope be made available to contemporary man, who so desperately needs it? Following the lead of Ernst Bloch, the German Marxist philosopher, who found that "biblical eschatology deals with what is central in human existence," [41] they affirm that "the key to human existence is to be found in the hopes which man holds for the future state of humanity and the world." [42] Man is "he-who-hopes," an eschatological being who is lured into the openness of the future with a "vision of the not-yet." Eschatology is transmuted into a phenomenology of hope, in other words, and it is this which provides a point of contact between the Biblical promise of the Kingdom of God and modern man.

Hope, of course, has invariably to do with the "new" and with the "future," so these too become root metaphors by which to understand not only the Christian faith with more perceptive accuracy but also man, history, God, and Reality itself. For instance, Pannenberg believes that the terms "hope," "self-fulfillment," "resurrection," "future life," "are not imposed upon men through a revelation from the outside, but are rooted in the nature of man's very being. . . . In a sense . . . hope is the voice of man's 'essential' (Tillich) or 'authentic' (Bultmann) being." [43] Man is called into being, and into the future, by the dynamic of hope. This is the creating, sustaining, and world-making force in him.

But eschatological hope is not only a clue to man's nature and his fulfillment, it is also a key to all history and its fulfillment. As seen in Jesus Christ it "has far-reaching significance for the interpretation of all history as God's history. This eschaton casts a light on the entirety of world history and its destiny." [44] "The end of history is present proleptically in Jesus of Nazareth." [45] Hope in his resurrection is not hope in the return of a resurrected individual, it is viewing history in its ultimate culmination. Hence it is a "world-historical event of eschatological significance," [46] which gives us the final perspective from which to judge world history.

The category of hope also provides a basic perspective of theological reflection on the nature of God, the God who "meets us out of the future." "The question of God is not the question of the existence of some remote infinite being. It is the question of the possibility of hope." [47] Hope for the future "is a hope and trust in God as the power of the future." [48] " 'God appears,' " says Moltmann, " 'as the power of the future to contradict the negative moments of existence that we now experience and to set free the forces through which victory is achieved. Only in the real transformation of an individual life and of the conditions of life by breaking the bonds of the present, and in essential change, does this freedom penetrate the history that its future lays open for it.' " [49] "The future is not only to be thought of subjectively as the referent of man's hope to transcend the given in his present, but as ontologically grounded in God's own mode of being." [50] God *is* the power of the future; to have hope in the open future is to have hope in God. The future has power over the present; so God has power over the present in the same way. He is the Source of creative advance. In this way creation and eschatology are united: the expectation and hope of the New Age, and the constant process of creation of the New by the future made present. God is the future of every past and present occasion, and "ontologically prior in his futurity to every event and epoch at the remotest distance from us." [51]

And, lastly, as gathered from the statements above, while Christian hope is usually connected with the risen Christ and the Coming Kingdom, it is now regarded as a structure of perception of reality in general, and as an ontological quality of all Being. The question of hope becomes the question of "the adequacy and the finality of the categories of human understanding." [52] Man hopes, but it is Hope, as the ontological structure of all Futures, that makes man.

Time does not allow a full discussion of the content of the rich ideas that flow from these seminal thinkers. It is all very heady stuff, indeed. I can only offer a sample sniff of the cork, so to speak, to give some idea, for comparison's sake, of what this newest ferment is about. Theological connoisseurs and those thirsting for further stimulation will have to go to the presses personally to savor the full-bodied flavor of the various vintages: Bloch '59 (*Das Prinzip Hoffnung*); Pannenberg '64 (*Grundzuge der Christologie*); Metz '65 (*Zur Theologie der Welt*); and Moltmann '67 (*Theologie der Hoffnung*).

Schweitzer's scholarly efforts a half century ago make him a part of the present secular translation of the religious questions for our age which both the Radicals and the theologians of Hope have reclaimed. Modern man is less interested in, and less tied to, the past than in former times, and any theology that does not look with concern at the present, and openly face with the age more toward the future, will be left in a traditional past which it worships as something quite unessential to our burgeoning needs. But even if Christianity and the church, and indeed religion itself, should wither away, like a Marxist state, the questions that it tried, however unsuccessfully, to answer, would still stand as ominously and persistently as ever before, if not more so, and how we answer them will, as in the past, determine our future. Theologians today are becoming more aware that *homo sapiens* is also, more than ever, *homo viator,* and that man is weary of listening to theories *about* the world but desires, in the words of Marx, to *change* the world. For he knows if he does not, it will change him, for change, controlled or uncontrolled, seems his only constant. "One truth stands firm," notes Schweitzer. "All that happens in world history rests on something spiritual [i.e., human passion, faith, energy, insight, and will]. If the spiritual is strong, it creates world history. If it is weak, it suffers world history. The question is, shall we make world history or only suffer it passively? . . . Shall we again win ideals that will have power over reality? This is the question before us today." [53] But this is not the only question. What kind of future, if any, can I expect? and, What can I hope for? are also disturbing questions that man today asks. In times past, Christianity could answer them with assurance; now it falters and stammers. It has no balm for these wounds of existence; the healing strength of its ancient ointments has dissipated. Its Kingdom is an unreal, far-off event; its eschatological hope is a mythological appendage; its answers are not in tune with the present diapasons of change. Behind its optimistic mask, says Schweitzer, hides a pessimistic face. Both Schweitzer and the theologians of Hope realize the urgent need for realistic answers, not palliatives. "What a task it will be to break the fetters of unthinking optimism and unthinking pessimism which hold us prisoners, and so to do what will pave the way of the renewal of civilization!" [54]

"In religion," Schweitzer writes, "we try to find an answer to the elementary questions with which each one of us is newly confronted every morning, namely, what meaning and what value is to be ascribed to our life: What am I in the world? What is my purpose in it? *What may I hope for in this world?*" [55] Schweizter's own attempt to answer these questions differs in language, style, and orientation, indeed, from the attempts of the theologians of Hope, but it is noteworthy how close he comes in anticipating many of the themes and ideas now current in their thought:

Again, after many centuries, the Kingdom of God has become a live question. Again mankind as a whole is changing its mind as to what it really means.

Modern faith finds the beginning of the Kingdom of God in Jesus and in the Spirit which came into the world with him. We no longer leave the fate of mankind to be decided at the end of the world. The time in which we live summons us to new faith in the Kingdom of God. . . . Mankind today must either realize the Kingdom of God or perish. The very tragedy of our present situation compels us to devote ourselves in faith to its realization. [56]

There appears, in the light of what has been said, several basic assumptions which Schweitzer, Bloch, Metz, Pannenberg, and Moltmann hold in common, despite their wide divergences of belief. They are: (1) that the Kingdom of God, in the words of Moltmann, "is not one element *of* Christianity, but it is the medium of Christian faith as such, the key in which everything is set, the glow that suffuses everything here in the dawn of an expected new day"; [57] (2) that the whole phenomenon of Biblical eschatological belief and hope offers us a clue, not just to an understanding of those particular periods of world history, but to a fathoming of the nature of man, God, society, and the whole sweep of history in the making; (3) that its essential thrust is to be interpreted as ideological, ethical, and spiritual; (4) that we must strive to regain its original fervor and impetus; (5) that this can, and must, be done; and that it can, and does, have vital meaning for our time; (6) that a depth reinterpretation of it involves us in the discussion of a phenomenology and ontology of hope; (7) that the world is an unfolding process in constant change, and hence hierarchical-static structures of thought are inadequate to characterize it; (8) that man is a constantly created and creating phenomenon; (9) that he has the capacity freely to initiate decisions and choices, by reason of the fact that (10) he is open to the future and the future is open to him; and (11) that hope and love spring from some source of which he is co-creative part, far deeper and more cosmic in scope than his own personal instincts.

Schweitzer's interpretation of the Kingdom of God is essentially spiritual. This he makes explicit, particularly when he speaks of it in relation to Jesus and Paul as a New Testament scholar. He moves it from the cosmological and theological to the ethical; from the outer and beyond, to the inner and between. But there is an ontological dimension to it also, which is hidden in his philosophy. Just as he refrains from using the terms "God," "love," and "religious faith," but speaks instead of the "Universal Will-to-Live," "reverence for life," and "world- and life-affirmation," when he addresses a wider audience as a philosopher, so he avoids the religious expression "Kingdom of God." He speaks rather of the Will-to-Live as it appears within human life as the Will-to-relatedness or -unity striving to overcome the *Selbstentzweiung,* or division, of life and world, man and world, life and life. The Kingdom of God is seen as a growing community of concerned men held in a fellowship of reverence for life, a fellowship that is bound by the actualization and enhancement of the Universal Will-to-Love in their lives. This aspect of the Cosmic Will, in religious terms, can be called "God"; its essential proclivity can be called the urge-to-relatedness, or, in Tillich's words, "the drive toward the reunion of the separated"; the imperative which it creates in us as persons can be called the desire to do the "Will of God"; and the visionary aim, or overall result, can be called the Kingdom of God, which ideally and always stands over against us as the challenge and inspiration of the Future.

The fulfillment of at-one-ness is our hope, an eschatological hope of the future, when the Will-to-unity or -love will be "all in all," and the enigma of the *Selbstentzweiung,* or cosmic estrangement, will be overcome. Meanwhile we live in the hope and the power of this Future—which, because we are part of the Universal Will-to-Live, is a present reality—and strive with the Spirit of love to become united ethically and spiritually with all Life. This hope is the power of the Will-to-relatedness moving within us; it does not move as fully, if at all, in the world, but in us *into* the world. Through our acts of spirit, the Future is made present, the beyond is absorbed by the present, to use Schweitzer's phrase. Ontologically it is the constant actualization of the potential of our full humanity, or authentic or essential natures. Our hope is *in,* and comes *from,* the living nowness of the Not-Yet. Without this Ground of creative potentiality and its constant luring of all things into being, there would be no life, no present, no reality. This is for Schweitzer the essence of the Kingdom of God, expressed philosophically in the language of his ethical pantheism and mixed with the idioms of the Theology of Hope.

In attempting to explain the unresolved conflict in his thought which exists between theism and pantheism, Schweitzer employs a most interesting simile.

There is an ocean-cold water without motion. In this ocean, however, is the Gulf Stream—hot water, flowing from the Equator towards the Pole. Enquire of all the scientists how it is physically imaginable that a stream of hot water flows between the waters of the ocean, which, so to speak, form its banks, the moving within the motionless; the hot within the cold: no scientist can explain it. Similarly there is the God of Love within the God of the Forces of the Universe—one with Him, and yet so totally different. We let ourselves be seized and carried away by that vital stream.[58]

This vital stream, flowing into the present from the measureless newness of the Future, is that which creates and nourishes our hope for the Kingdom of God among men.

Schweitzer is not overly optimistic about man's future. He knows a social or cosmic upheaval, particularly with the power man now possesses, could easily end life on earth as we know it.[59] But he is not pessimistic. Since "no other destiny awaits mankind than that which, through its mental and spiritual disposition, it prepares for itself," [60] there is reason for hope. And it is to this that he addresses himself as he seeks, in his radical theology, to provide a reasoned basis for hope.

Albert Camus, the late French author-playwright, like Schweitzer was pessimistic of knowledge per se ever bringing any easy solutions for the absurd forlornness of man's exile in existence. He too saw the chasm "between the mind that desires and the world that disappoints," and knew that the human voyager had only the compass of his own mind and heart to rely upon. He too rejected the spurious abstractions of superficial supernaturalisms. Yet even he could say before his untimely death, " 'In the middle of winter I at last discovered that there was in me an invincible summer!' " [61]

But Schweitzer does not stop here. He moves stubbornly on to discover the basis for this "invincible summer" in the invincible Universal Will-to-Love that seeks to bind all life together. His spiritual life is as a tree planted by the rivers of water which never run dry. It is Schweitzer's hope that our age may find in the midst of its winter eternal summer—the Kingdom of God—so that the barren wood of Christianity may become once again a green forest of hope for man.

VII

Schweitzer and the Future of Belief

" 'Is RELIGION A FORCE in the spiritual life of our age?' " asks Schweitzer. "I answer, in your name and mine, 'No!' There is still religion in the world; there is much religion in the church; there are many pious people among us. Christianity can still point to works of love and to social works of which it can be proud. There is a longing for religion among many who no longer belong to the churches. I rejoice to concede this. And yet we must hold fast to the fact that religion is not a force." [1] When it sanctioned the wars and "joined forces with the spirit of the world," it was the "one victim of defeat." "And that religion *was* defeated," declares Schweitzer, "is apparent in our time. For it lifts up its voice but only to protest. It cannot command. The spirit of the age does not listen. It goes its own way." [2]

There are "two different currents" or kinds of religion, according to Schweitzer. One is "dogmatic," the other is "free from dogma": "Dogmatic religion is based on the creeds, the early church, and the reformation. It has no relations with thinking, but emphasizes the difference between thinking and believing. This religion . . . is more dominated by the thought of redemption than by that of the kingdom of God. It has no wish to influence the world." [3] "The religion free from dogma is to some extent the heir of rationalistic religion. It is ethical, limits itself to the fundamental ethical verities, and endeavours, so far as is in its power, to remain on good terms with thinking. It wants to realize something of the kingdom of God in the world. It believes itself identical with the religion of Jesus," because it believes that his was a nondogmatic religion, i.e., one which expressed something universal in the heart of man and which "can be adopted in any age." [4]

Christianity is not a force in the world today because it abdicated from its high calling to work freely and freeingly among men to bring in the Kingdom of Peace and Justice; it became more and more a religion of supernatural redemption and dogma.

Schweitzer is adamant that a nondogmatic religion need not be tied to any particular tradition, nor derive its impetus and inspiration from any sacred creed. The ethical and spiritual ideals, for example, of his religion of Reverence for Life overarch all religions and touch what is essential and common to all men. And it is man and life, not God, Christ, or church, that are important. As we have seen, Schweitzer does not extol Jesus as the "Lord of our lives" because his life and teachings are recorded in sacred scripture, nor because he believes Jesus was some superterrestrial being whom Christians worship as the Son of God. It is because of the universal ideals which he exhibited that make him worthy of exemplification for all men. And this is one of the tests and hallmarks of a nondogmatic religion.

Ernst Troeltsch perceived that historic periods, where the old is giving way to new eras yet unborn, are the most active and creative, as well as the most disturbing, of all epochs. This is certainly true of our time. Today we exist in an interregnum between the collapse of one ideological style of culture and the rise of a new. Ernst Bloch speaks of our contemporary world as *Zwischen den Zeiten*, between the ages, or a period of *Zeitwende*. In every aspect of life we are experiencing upsetting and momentous changes. It is a period of split foundations and collapsing superstructures, of challenge and ferment, of retreat and retrenchment. Our views of society, politics, language, values, customs, man, history, space—all are radically changing. Indeed, dislocation seems to be modern man's metaphor.

As we have determined, this is no less true of religion. Theologians are cognizant, as Schweitzer was fifty years ago, that Christianity has lost its power, and they are searching, as he did, for new foundations of belief and new locations for action. But how far have they actually been willing to go in fashioning an adequate, "free," religion for our times? or, in fulfilling the desperate need for rethinking our value systems?

The need for rethinking our religious answers, as well as our problems, is obvious, and I applaud the present ferment; but, to be quite frank, viewing the whole theological scene I am puzzled and wearied by the furor. Why, one wonders, is so much energy and enthusiasm being spent again on interpreting, reinterpreting, arguing for, defending, reworking, and renewing the various theological beliefs and concepts when such internal and external housecleaning, foundation-patching, and new-addition-building have been so traditional in each age? Once again Christianity, chameleon-wise, is straining to make itself "new," "relevant," "challenging," "prophetic," "dynamic," struggling to revitalize its symbols, to offer a "new" cure for a sick humanity, to rediscover the "real" Christ, or the "true" meaning of the cross, Bible, God, or church. With all too few exceptions, this is old hat. One feels like Martin Marty, who was reported to have begun a talk on the death of God, when it first appeared, with: "Oh, well, here we go again."

It is difficult enough to find answers, even partial ones, to the nerve-racking, demanding, and difficult problems which we as humans face in the last half of the twentieth century, without complicating and confounding the issues by continually having to find them within the narrow Christian framework. It is not always a freeing and helpful procedure, at best; to have to present our answers before the bar of Christian faith and judgment is tedious and tendentious.

It is difficult to unlearn, even in the face of the few contemporary exceptions in Radical theology, that however Christian theologians mix their theology with secular ideas, modern philosophy, scientific discoveries, depth psychology, new left politics, absurdist drama, or with Blake, Camus, Heidegger, Ayre, Freud, Marx—or whomsoever—it still always comes out minted in "Christian" coinage whether it is stamped "In God We Trust" or "Jesus Saves" or not. We all know the name of the game is theology and that there are certain commitments that go with the apologetic procedures, but these are the very things that are bothersome and under question. In order to keep things "Christian," theologians always have to commit the fallacy of special exemption regardless of how open-, new-, secular-, scientific-, philosophical-, or universal-sounding their words are. There is nothing a Christian theologian relishes more, it seems, than a chance to defend the faith again against new upheavals and attacks; the more heretical the better. For it only becomes a challenge to his imagination and hermeneutic talents as to how to reinterpret the "Gospel" in modern-sounding terminology and new thought styles and *still* remain within the "Faith." This is always possible, of course, regardless of how far he strays, for he merely reinterprets his terms as he goes—even the term "faith," if need be—in order to "prove" that the "true" essence of Christianity is still the only way, or at least the only live option, to save mankind, or solve its problems, or assure man of "authentic existence." There seems no end to his inventiveness for discovering new sleight-of-mind tricks to say the same things in new ways, or new things in the old Biblical way. His circumlocutions are positively ingenious. They match the modern literary critics' facility for inventing new levels of depth meaning and symbol interpretation in the plainest of passages where everything esoterically becomes fraught with hidden significance. Nothing seems to daunt him; no hard facts, no counterquestions nor arguments can be cited to deter him from his appointed hermeneutic rounds; he merely absorbs them, reinterprets them in his favor, or sidesteps them in such a way everyone believes he has fully taken them into account. Show him some new life-style or social change, for example, and in time he will find a way to argue that they *really* are Christian in the first place, and that they were anticipated by Moses, Christ, or Kerygma. He will invent terms—invariably written in capitals and charged with ultimacy—if he runs into difficulty, reshaping not only the Christian message but reality as well to fit whatever challenge he faces.

It is all very persuasive. The theologian today, for instance, will explain to you how "faith" must be recast in accordance with reason, tested by fact, or, to make it sound more radical, eliminated altogether. And yet when pushed into the precincts of his last evasion by logic, reason, and the honesty which he proclaims, he replies, "It is an affair of faith," or "personal decision," or "It is a paradox." Or *worse*, he employs the autobiographical cop-out: while assuming to be a part of the scholarly community's truthward quest for general and shareable knowledge, he replies, when pressed for evidence or proof, "This, of course, is *only* how *I* see it"! This is supposed to allow him to have his cake of immunity from all the hard tests of critical analysis, and partake of the sweet rewards of his scholarly pose at the same time. Such theologians have not learned to distinguish between being *personally* involved in doing theology, and being *privately* involved.

When historians note the importance of certain key events and/or personages in history and speak of them as influential or even revolutionary, everyone understands and, more or less, places them into the usual perspective; viz., the Battle of Hastings, the invention of the printing press, Darwin's *Origin of Species*, etc., are regarded as events that truly changed the face of history.

Yet when theologians speak about the life of Jesus, and the rise of Christianity, usually it is not regarded in the same manner, but is distorted out of shape by religious fervor or faith's eagerness to try to make it more than it ever was, or can be. Suddenly it becomes transformed on to a transhistorical or suprahistorical level, or interpreted in ways no respectable historian would devise. Even when theologians strain to be good historians, they cannot contain themselves, and their religious imaginations gain an upper hand; the facts are tampered with and the evidence is heightened in order to make them beg the question for faith's sake, or Christ's sake. This, of course, is legitimized by such terms as *Heilsgeschichte*.

If the historic event of Jesus remained as it should within the same purview as all other important, catalytic events in history—despite the problems we find surrounding historical methodology, interpretation, and the historical imagination, there would still be enough mystery surrounding it to satisfy the most committed and imaginative theologian. The historic, secular event of Jesus and the early church is still fraught with unusual import, even when compared with other culture-changing movements. Why do we always need an extra theological twist to heighten its significance? Does this not show the poverty of the Christian sensibility, or reveal something about Christianity's lack of security and courage?

I agree with Dewart: If one allows the principle that all truth is implicit in the Bible, or in the kerygma of the Bible, or in Jesus Christ, "one can with circular safety project whatever truth one learns from the present into one's philosophical past. No error will ever be found. No shadow of doubt, distortion or limitation will threaten. All new found truths are *ex post facto* to the event." [5]

When a Christian theologian today says he rejects everything Biblical, even disbelieves in God, and wants to negate the entire tradition—take heed. More times than not there is bound to be a trick in the offing. Suddenly, he puts them all back, he restores them all even though they may be disguised in very strange dress. And if you look closely, beneath his secular, literary, dialectical surface—you will find the metaphysical Christ peeking back at you. For indubitably, "Jesus Christ is the same yesterday, today, and forevermore" because the Christian theologian, by definition, will never let you forget it, and by the fallacy of special exemption, will never let it be otherwise.

If Christianity is to become once again a force in the spiritual life of mankind, then it is going to have to give up not only its mythological world view, its dogmatic schemes of salvation, its authoritarian compulsion, but its smug exclusivity and its uses of the fallacy of special exemption as well.

Schweitzer's thought is not above criticism, by any means. It has its own particular factual and logical defects. But being theologically dogmatic, and exclusively Christian in a *sub rosa* sense, is not one of them. His radical theology, if it does anything, calls upon us first, to become men, and second, Christians, if at all. Regardless of how much a part of the Christian tradition he is, regardless of how often he speaks of Jesus, God, Christ, Bible, Spirit, Kingdom of God, etc., his thought escapes the tendentious and question-begging manner that usually infects the Christian theologian's method of approach. This is one of the reasons his thought coalesces more readily with the insights of other world religions and with the contemporary mind.

Following the lead of Schweitzer's thought, we realize that the world is too vast and multidimensional to be perceived only through the neat, tiny spectacles of the Judeo-Christian tradition. God is too great to squeeze any longer into the Christian molds of theistic or Christocentric thought. Man is too complex and protean to catch on the creedal pins of a Christian interpretation for full understanding. This point of view reflects the prophetic protests against dogmatic religion of both Schweitzer and the Radicals.

There are, however, several interesting differences between them which I would like to point out.

Maynard Kaufman finds that Radical theology is "divided into two types": those in metaphysics who talk about God without any Christocentric hang-up, and those in secular theology "who do a kind of glorified cultural anthropology," who talk about Christ without any God or metaphysics. "It used to be possible to talk about God most adequately by talking about Christ. But now these two doctrines seem to be incompatible. Theologians who talk about God find it difficult to talk about Christ or the Jesus of History, while theologians who talk about Jesus or Christ claim it is unnecessary to worry about God."[6] While the latter are more involved with problems of social ethics and cultural anthropology, claiming Jesus as primary, the former, he believes, are more consistent and capable of doing constructive theology. Though both "work toward an erasure of the distinction between the sacred and the profane,"[7] the secular theologians (such as Cox) promote "a process of desacralization," while the post-Christian atheists (such as Altizer) and the philosophical theists (such as John Cobb, Jr.) "are in quest of the sacred" within the profane. Altizer immanentizes the Sacred into the profane world by his kenotic theory of Christ, and Cobb, following Whitehead's philosophy, emphasizes that the "needless bifurcation between nature and history is no longer necessary because nature is conceived of as a process which includes man and history."[8]

Kaufman applauds the attempt of Radical theology to overcome the false split between God and the world, the sacred and the secular, but he insists that "a commitment to the secular . . . does not automatically rule out the relevance of every metaphysical philosophy to theological thought."[9] He is definitely on the side of those theologians who _do_ still take the question of God seriously, but do so without returning to traditional theistic concepts, falling back into a dualistic view of God and the world, clinging to a soteriological view of Christ or Jesus, "absolutizing the profane historical process,"[10] or collapsing religion into an "inconsistent affirmation of secularity" with its "superfluous justification of the _status quo_."[11] In his opinion those theologians who are following the leads of such seminal thinkers as Whitehead, Hartshorne, and Berdyaev stand the best chance of accomplishing this.

As I tried to place Schweitzer in Kaufman's schema (and I

failed completely), it struck me that Schweitzer bridges both types of Radical theology, or more accurately, all three groups which Kaufman mentions—the secular theologians, the post-Christian atheists, and the process philosophers—and does so without falling into some of their excesses or weaknesses.

First, Schweitzer speaks of Jesus, as we have seen, as the spiritual exemplar of our ethical wills, but without being theologically trapped in a Christocentric predicament or recasting him in a soteriological role. Man attains authentic existence, if you will, by creative acts and not by the grace of God in Christ.

Kaufman finds that most of the Radical theologians are inconsistent at this point. They espouse a nonsoteriological form of Christianity, but in time slip back into casting Jesus as "the center of their thought." "Although they may have given up all theories of the atonement except the moral-influence theory, their Christianity remains soteriological. . . . Jesus may not be regarded as a divine archetype, but he functions as a Christ figure whose image redeems the time in which we wait. This is still a redemptive function, but with the difference that the Christ figure now serves to give sanction to secular or popular culture." [12]

I presume Schweitzer would be included by him in this indictment, but the distinctions are not fine enough for me to do so without reservations. It seems to me that redeeming through moral example and redeeming mankind by a special act of God are two different things. It all depends on how one defines the term "redeem," and Kaufman has considerably stretched its theological applicability. I do not find that Jesus functions as a "Christ figure" for Schweitzer even in Kaufman's sense; unless, of course, Berdyaev, whom Kaufman admires, and whose thought he hopes will help to redeem man from the tyranny of history, among other things, is therefore a Christ figure to him. I am not being facetious. I am trying to say that everyone who admires Jesus and takes him as the one to whom one repairs is not falling into a Christian soteriology necessarily. Such a criticism depends upon precisely determining the role and function of Jesus in the person's *entire* scheme of thought.

Schweitzer, in the second place, combines elements of the antimetaphysical bias of the secular radicals with a definite metaphysical involvement, as seen in his development of the philosophy of Will-to-Live, which places him in the company of the process theologians.

As I admitted in Chapter III, this is a strange but, to me, felicitous inconsistency. Kaufman notes the secular theologians "are likely to reject metaphysics for religious and theological rather than philosophical reasons," [13] and I believe this is more or less true of Schweitzer. He is a *kind* of theist, in other words, without being stuck in the airy abstractions of a religious metaphysic or the exaggerated claims of a theistic faith. These are the reasons some of the Radicals believe that the God question is unimportant and best dispensed with. Just what kind he is, is difficult to determine, particularly when he admits he stands inconsistently between pantheism and theism and never bothered to resolve them. His philosophy of ethical pantheism is as far as he felt it was necessary to go in rationally grounding his ethic of Reverence for Life in a world view.

Charles Hartshorne, the foremost interpreter of Whitehead, and an outstanding philosopher in his own right, claims that his philosophy of "surrelativism" or "panentheism" is compatible with pantheism. [14] Taking Schweitzer's unfinished but provocative philosophy of the Will-to-Live, I am sure his views would have been, in many instances, in agreement with Hartshorne's panentheism, had he pursued further the dilemma of being caught between theism and pantheism. Hartshorne's kind of theism would, I believe, have been more acceptable to Schweitzer had he known of it. I say this because Schweitzer was too much of a vitalist, or process thinker, to be happy with any traditional form of theism. But of course Schweitzer gave up the quest as hopeless; and, as we have determined, his interests lay in what he strongly felt were more fruitful directions.

Clark detects Schweitzer's affinity to Whiteheadian thought also. Schweitzer's

> conception of the cosmos as being seeking reunion with itself has . . . contemporary parallels in the philosophy of Whitehead and the theology of Tillich.[14a]

I am convinced that Schweitzer's notion of reverence for all forms of life has greatest significance in this ontological context, since the ontological approach views all beings as sharing the same qualitative status as manifestations of Being itself.

But even more promising than Schweitzer's reverence for life as a fruitful application of his call for self-devotion, and as a corollary to Tillich's ontology of love, is the doctrine of a co-creatorship. The idea of co-creatorship is implicit in Schweitzer's references to man's destiny as "an active, purposeful force in the world," and in his mention of "our cooperation with the activity which the world-spirit wills for us." Whitehead states the doctrine explicitly:

> God is in the world . . . creating in us and around us. Insofar as man partakes of that creative process does he partake of the divine of God. . . . His true destiny as co-creator in the universe is his dignity and his grandeur.

God is creating the world in us as will-to-love which seeks to minimize and make progressively less prevalent the clash of will-to-live against will-to-live which characterizes the estrangement of existence. We participate in that creative process, and therefore in God, insofar as we will and live love. The very attitude of compassion is intrinsically valuable, for there are many instances of will-to-live estranged from itself which we are powerless to prevent or heal, and in such cases all we can do is to feel the pain of the conflict, where not to do so would be to blunt ourselves.[15]

I add this, not only because I think Clark is warranted in finding a significant parallel, which invites expansion, between Schweitzerian and Whiteheadian thought, but to demonstrate how Schweitzer anticipates both prongs of radical theology: Christian atheism and non-Christian theism.

Thirdly, because of his ethical pantheism, Schweitzer immanentizes the sacred into the world. He emphasizes as do all three groups the present, the here and now, the betweenness of men, and the importance of a this-worldly focusing of our ethical and creative energies. But he does so without deifying the secular world, or absolutizing history. He does not agree one has to write the obituary of all forms of transcendence in order to affirm life and humanity. His radical theology avoids both the tyranny of traditional transcendence on the one hand, and the autocratic, historical man of scientific humanism on the other. Man is autonomous, but he is part of a potentially wider realm of Being than he is often aware. As Gabriel Fackre astutely noted, many of the Radical theologians have a distorted, biased view of transcendence, a term that can be and has been defined in many ways—not all of them inconsistent with Radical theology's emphasis upon the this-worldliness of the Christian message.[16] It can still consistently be used in connection with a nondualistic world view, for transcendence can mean transsituational, transindividual, transhistorical, noncapricious, intrasubjective, and universally recognizable.[17] It is one of the weaknesses of secular theology that it has not taken these alternatives into a serious consideration, but is still stuck by its prejudice to only one traditional, and outmoded, form.

Also, Schweitzer avoids secular theology's "bondage to the givenness and facticity of history," [18] which Kaufman describes as one of its most pernicious errors. It got rid of one absolute, the transcendent God, only to acclaim another, Christian history. This is to be expected, perhaps, since Christianity is a historical faith; but the secular theologian, "still informed by that truncated theology which says God (or Something Ultimate) is active in history, views with indiscriminate seriousness whatever comes to pass." [19] "Thus," writes Kaufman, "he is committed to what Christianity has become in its historical development and seeks only to rationalize the result than change it or acknowledge its bankruptcy." [20] This identification of the sacred with secular history overlooks, among other things, the eschatological nature of the Christian message, which in turn has been distorted by a projection of our modern concerns into the life and teachings of Jesus, as van Buren has done, giving them a purely secular meaning: a procedure that Schweitzer would find to be a violation of the historical method and a gross misinterpretation of fact. Schweitzer and many others, including Bultmann, have reminded us that Jesus "preached the coming of the Kingdom of God as an eschatological consummation, and his human life was lived toward that end." [21] This could hardly be called a sanctioning of the secular world. "There is a world of difference," Kaufman validly points out, "between a doctrine of the incarnation which sanctions secularity and the incarnate life of Jesus with its eschatological orientation. In view of this it is hard to imagine that the secular theologians would affirm secularity and worldliness, or, as Cox does, that 'technopolis' is the long-awaited Kingdom of God." [22]

Schweitzer makes it explicit that we can expect nothing from history. The creative and religious spirit is not called forth, nor sustained, by historical facts. Christianity does not rest upon history, but upon the mighty ethical and life-affirming spirit that "streams forth from . . . [Jesus] and flows through our time also," which he says, "can neither be shaken nor confirmed by any historical discovery." [23] Schweitzer's ethical mysticism is founded upon a cosmic, not a historical, consciousness which he tries to instill in his radical theology by means of a spiritual, not a historical, interpretation of the Kingdom of God. For these reasons, Schweitzer can be included in that group of thinkers, along with Berdyaev, Eliade, Norman O. Brown, and Herbert Marcuse, who speak of the constrictions of Western man's historical consciousness, and the necessity of freeing it from the tyrannies of historicism. He would agree with Berdyaev, for example, who argues that spirit " 'must be freed and purified from the power of the historical, or, to speak more truly, from the power of historicism, from the process of making what is relative absolute.' " [24]

Besides foreshadowing many of the recent theological trends, combining pertinent elements of the Radical theologies, including process theology, and avoiding some of the errors of a "dogmatic religion" which persistent critics of the New Christianity have elaborated, Schweitzer's thought is important and relevant today for other reasons.

One I have already mentioned. It is that Schweitzer has the rare ability to enhance the essential ideas of the Christian religion without becoming its special pleader, compressing or stretching every idea, fact, and trend to fit its forms of thought. His kind of religious outlook and dedication does not reinforce, but pulls down, traditional barriers between it and other religions, and the world. In an age of increasing ideological polarization, religious tribalism, and social alienation, I find this resolve more than an intellectual nicety. It is becoming increasingly mandatory.

Our world is in too volatile a state to permit falsehoods and precious half-truths to continue to live, however traditional and revered, among us and work their poisonous effects. We must become more honest about our own intellectual shortcomings and more magnanimous toward those we find in others. We must become ethical enough in our intellectual pursuits as well, to allow deep thought to ply its trade openly in every level of life. It alone can bring the wider perspectives which are the only correctives for the provincialism, divisive intolerance, fanaticism, and truncated views which are a major source of confusion and misery. Without the purging discipline of intellectual fairness and honesty man may destroy himself in unbridled excess and arrogant blindness.

Secondly, Schweitzer is important to the Christian believer today, for in moving into a new era—a post-Christian era, as it is called—the experiences and insights of one who has studied and reveres Christianity's past, who is part of its symbol system, is molded by its hopes, nurtured by its visions, and yet has broken with its center, are invaluable. The agnostic in Christ, the atheist in the church, the secularist in divine service, the seeker of the sacred beside others in the midst of the profane—all are new experiences for us, and we need as much guidance and help as possible as we venture through the *Zeitwende* into the world of tomorrow with its new forms of religious consciousness and commitment. Unlike so many of our great minds, Schweitzer shares the concerns of both the modern world and the Christian church without being submerged in, or by, either.

"Christopher Dawson," writes Alex Vidler, "once observed that 'men today are divided between those who have kept their spiritual roots and lost their contact with the existing order of society, and those who have preserved their social contact and lost their spiritual roots.' " [25] Schweitzer is one exception to this, for he kept both. In a time in which many have lost one or the other, or emphasized one to the exclusion of the other, as some theologians have done, or, what is even more likely, lost both, Schweitzer's accomplishment is something worthy of serious study.

Thirdly, Schweitzer is theologian enough to fully appreciate the subtleties and significance of the theological enterprise, but philosopher enough to demand the sober clarity and hesitancy of philosophic thought that is often essential in the face of the exuberant and emotive claims of the theologian.

And, too, Schweitzer is scientist enough, having studied and practiced medicine, to be enthused by science's models of thought and convinced of the imperative necessity of its precise methods of description, prediction, and control, but astute enough not to fall into scientism, by turning it into an ideological panacea.

Another way in which Schweitzer's thought is relevant for the development of future forms of belief is that he saw the necessity of combining the thought of East and West. And this he tried to do. He was wise enough to realize that these forms of thought need each other. Each lacks what the other can give. The problem was not to prove the superiority of one over the other, he realized, but to remedy them so that "a more perfect and powerful form of thought" could emerge "to be shared in common by all mankind." [26] He tried to collate their most pertinent and penetrating perceptions in the name of man—not in the name of Christianity or the West. In this he was truly a prophet, as I believe the future will prove.

Lastly, though it is recognized that Schweitzer was prophetic and innovative in most every field he entered, many believe that an appreciation of the revolutionary character of the upheavals that were occurring in modern society was lacking. He may be a forerunner of some of the radical ideas now alive in religion, so the argument runs, but his conception of the dynamics of cultural change is derived from a nineteenth-century bourgeois point of view. To disabuse the minds of those who hold this opinion, I offer the following quotation from an editorial in the *Church Messenger* he wrote in 1920:

Today the clergyman expects that the Church will provide him with the means of livelihood. It will do so to an ever diminishing extent. *We are moving towards a complete revolution of society. The old ideas about everything, from the family to private property, are changing. Productive work is now the law for all.* In this new ordering of society there will be no room for professions whose representatives appear as idlers. If the churches can no longer support their clergy, it is a sign that the clergy are no longer capable of maintaining the Church as a prosperous institution.

The parson as an officer of the Church has outlived his usefulness. He must engage in new evangelical experiments. . . . The minister must be capable of performing this service for his people and thus setting an example of productive work. Moreover this would be nothing new but simply a return to the original sources and spirit of primitive Christianity.[27]

This remark, "calculated to promote a downright revolution in the conception of a professional clergy," presages another more recent pronouncement on the role of the church in society by Bonhoeffer, which makes for an interesting comparison:

The Church is her true self only when she exists for humanity. As a fresh start she should give away all her endowments to the poor and needy. The clergy should live solely on the free-will offerings of their congregations, or possibly engage in some secular calling. . . . She must not underestimate the importance of human example, which has its origin in the humanity of Jesus, and which is so important in the teaching of St. Paul. It is not abstract argument, but concrete example which gives her word emphasis and power.[28]

Both Schweitzer's and Bonhoeffer's statements are ahead of their time and cause considerable consternation to most Christians who read them, particularly those who grasp the implications of what is actually being said. But Christianity must be fully aware of the coming social revolution and be prepared to become an enlightened contributor to it, or perish. Radical movements are tolerable, even stimulating, so long as they are confined to questions of belief. But when they are directed toward changes in the social patterns of life and our concrete behavior, they become something else again. When the time comes for theory to be changed into practice, and knowledge transformed into experience, most learn the meaning of the word "radical" for the first time. Perhaps the most radical aspect of Schweitzer still rests on what he did, not on what he said. We know too few who personally put into action what they theoretically proposed, such as Schweitzer who authored with his life the above prophetic quotation.

To an age incredulous of theology, disillusioned with science and technological progress, uninspired and weary with the ideals of humanism, the timely and challenging thought of Schweitzer may have strong appeal. To Christianity it must have a strong appeal, if it is to avoid remaining a "dogmatic," and become a "free" and freeing, religious force. His open-ended philosophy of life, his religion of ethical pantheism, his mystical affirmation of all Life as One, his ethic of the inviolability of all life, his sketches for the future of hope, are at least fraught with the possibilities for conceptual and revolutionary renewal.

One day while I was speaking with the late Willard Sperry, dean of Harvard Divinity School, he made the prophetic comment to me that in his opinion Schweitzer's religion of reverence for life is simple and at the same time profound enough to become in the future a great and moving force in the world. He went on to say that in an age in which *irreverence* for life has become the dominant attitude, Schweitzer's reaffirmation of life in the spirit of true humanitarianism seems something more than important; it is a light that shines in the darkness, and whether the darkness comprehends it or not, it helps to fill the vast, impersonal emptiness of our technological age with renewed meaning and hope.

This book has tried to show that Schweitzer is a prophet of Radical Christianity. In conclusion, let me list again the similarities I find that substantiate this: his rejection of orthodox Christianity; his radical intellectual honesty at all costs; his rejection of theological and metaphysical attempts to solve man's tangled problems; his seeing the limitations of Biblical hermeneutics for meeting the difficulties of the new age; his refusal to theologize or rationalize away the unsolvable problems of suffering, pain, and evil; his demythologizing of the New Testament; his de-divinization of Jesus; his depersonalization of God as seen outside of man in the world; his implied consideration of the death of the absolute or the traditional God of Christianity; his immanentizing of the divine Spirit into the world via recasting the Sacred in semipantheistic terms, and moving beyond theism; his practical mysticism of actuality where the sacred dimension is created between man and man, and between man and all forms of life; his shift of emphasis in his theology from the soteriological to the creative; his strong humanistic and rationalistic strains in his thought; his open-ended method of doing theology which is mainly ethical and anthropological; his seeing the eschatological hope as the central, and not peripheral, insight of Christianity which is currently being revived; his existential involvement with the actual world and its sharp taste of reality; his syncretistic accommodation of knowledge and other religions outside Christianity; and his keeping Jesus as the paradigmatic master of our ethical wills.

Notes

Introduction

1. Thomas J. J. Altizer, ed., *Toward a New Christianity: Readings in the Death of God Theology* (Harcourt, Brace and World, Inc., 1967).

2. William R. Miller, ed., *The New Christianity* (Dell Publishing Co., Inc., 1967).

3. Altizer, ed., *Toward a New Christianity*, p. 14.

4. Altizer's letter to me, July 21, 1968.

5. John R. Everett, "Albert Schweitzer and Philosophy," *Social Research*, Vol. XXXIII, No. 4 (Winter, 1966), pp. 527 ff.

6. Fritz Buri, *Albert Schweitzer als Theologe heute* (Zurich: Verlagsverein Schaffhausen, 1955), p. 4.

7. Henry Clark, *The Ethical Mysticism of Albert Schweitzer* (Beacon Press, Inc., 1962), p. 167.

8. Charles R. Joy, "Introduction," in Albert Schweitzer, *The Psychiatric Study of Jesus*, tr. by C. R. Joy (Beacon Press, Inc., 1948), p. 17.

9. Jackson Ice, "Dr. Schweitzer at 90," *The Hibbert Journal*, Vol. LXIII, No. 249 (Winter, 1965), p. 72.

10. *Ibid.*, pp. 75–77.

11. Oskar Kraus, *Albert Schweitzer* (London: Adam & Charles Black, Ltd., 1944), p. 171.

12. Ernst Cassirer, "Albert Schweitzer as Critic of Nineteenth Century Ethics," in A. A. Roback, ed., *Albert Schweitzer Jubilee Book* (Sci-Art Publishers, 1945), p. 242.

13. Everett, *loc. cit.*, p. 513.

14. Albert Schweitzer, *Verfall und Wiederaufbau der Kultur* (Munich: C. H. Beck, 1923), p. 52.

15. Albert Schweitzer, *Out of My Life and Thought*, tr. by C. T.

Campion, p. 240. Copyright 1933, 1949, © 1961 by Holt, Rinehart and Winston, Inc. Used by permission of Holt, Rinehart and Winston, Inc.

16. Buri, *Albert Schweitzer als Theologe heute.*

17. From an interview reported in the Garrett Theological Seminary *Forum*, No. 1 (1965–1966).

18. See Tillich's and Hamilton's ideas on "waiting" and "silence," viz., Paul Tillich, *The Shaking of the Foundations* (Charles Scribner's Sons, 1948), pp. 149–152; William Hamilton, "Thursday's Child," in Thomas J. J. Altizer and William Hamilton, eds., *Radical Theology and the Death of God* (The Bobbs-Merrill Company, Inc., 1966), p. 92.

19. Gabriel Langfeldt, *Albert Schweitzer: A Study of His Philosophy of Life,* tr. by Maurice Michael (London: George Allen & Unwin, Ltd., 1960), p. 12.

20. Schweitzer, *Life and Thought*, p. 51.

21. E. N. Mozley, *The Theology of Albert Schweitzer* (The Macmillan Company, 1951), p. 113.

22. Norman Cousins, *Dr. Schweitzer of Lambaréné* (Harper & Brothers, 1960), p. 195. Copyright © 1960 by Norman Cousins. Used by permission of Harper & Row, Publishers, Inc.

23. *Ibid.*, pp. 190–191.

24. Mozley, *The Theology of Albert Schweitzer*, p. 115.

25. Albert Schweitzer, *Christianity and the Religions of the World,* tr. by Johanna Powers (Doubleday & Doran Company, Inc., 1923), p. 3.

26. George N. Marshall, *An Understanding of Albert Schweitzer* (Philosophical Library, Inc., 1966), p. 70.

27. When referring to the contemporary Radical theologians, I use a capital "R"; when using the term generally, a lowercase "r."

I. *Christian Revolutionary*

1. George Seaver, *Christian Revolutionary* (Harper & Brothers, 1944), p. 1.

2. *Ibid.*

3. Altizer, "America and the Future of Theology," in Altizer and Hamilton, eds., *Radical Theology*, p. 15.

4. Seaver, *Christian Revolutionary*, p. 124.

5. *Ibid.*

6. Kraus, *Albert Schweitzer*, p. 5.

7. John Middleton Murry, *Love, Freedom and Society* (London: Jonathan Cape, Ltd., 1957), p. 20.

8. *Ibid.*

9. Thomas J. J. Altizer, *The Gospel of Christian Atheism* (The Westminster Press, 1966), p. 9.

10. Murry, *Love, Freedom and Society,* p. 192. Italics mine.

11. Langfeldt, *Albert Schweitzer,* p. 14.

12. *Ibid.,* p. 115.

13. James Daane, "Sacrifice Without God," *Christianity Today,* Feb. 16, 1962, p. 44.

14. Seaver, *Christian Revolutionary,* p. 124.

15. Langfeldt, *Albert Schweitzer,* p. 115.

16. *Ibid.,* p. 10.

17. Identified, not joined.

18. This is strange since Schweitzer reacted strongly against the "liberal" school of theology. See John Wick Bowman, "From Schweitzer to Bultmann," *Theology Today,* Vol. XI, No. 2 (July, 1954), pp. 160 ff.

19. Marshall, *An Understanding of Albert Schweitzer,* pp. 120–121. Quoted matter refers to, respectively: Seaver, *Christian Revolutionary,* pp. 42–43; Erica Anderson, *The World of Albert Schweitzer* (Harper & Brothers, 1954), p. 109.

20. Langdon Gilkey, "The God Is Dead Theology and the Possibility of God Language," mimeographed lectures given at the University of Chicago Divinity School, Sept., 1964, p. 1.

21. See Martin Marty, *Varieties of Unbelief* (Holt, Rinehart and Winston, Inc., 1964), and Michael Novak, *Belief and Unbelief* (The Macmillan Company, 1965).

22. E. L. Mascall, *The Secularization of Christianity* (Holt, Rinehart and Winston, Inc., 1966), p. 6.

23. William Hamilton, "Questions and Answers on the Radical Theology," in Jackson Lee Ice and John J. Carey, eds., *The Death of God Debate* (The Westminster Press, 1967), p. 215.

24. *Ibid.,* p. 214.

25. Paul Tillich, *The New Being* (Charles Scribner's Sons, 1955), p. 19.

26. *Ibid.,* p. 24.

27. I disagree with Hamilton and Altizer that "atheist" is a more accurate term than "agnostic," necessarily. "Agnostic suggests maybe, and the 'death of God' is not a maybe theology," says Hamilton. My reply is, maybe it should be, for even he admits, "they are atheists with a difference" (Hamilton, "Questions and Answers on the Radical Theology," in Ice and Carey, eds., *The Death of God Debate,* p. 214). Schweitzer is an agnostic "with a difference." Also, Hamilton further qualifies the term by saying, "There is an

element of expectation, even hope, that removes my position from classical atheisms." (Hamilton, "The Death of God Theologies Today," in Altizer and Hamilton, eds., *Radical Theology*, p. 41.) Hope for what? Hope that "we might be enabled to stand before him once again." This is a strange form of atheism. Agnosticism is capable of including the possibility of hope just as strongly; and it involves just as rigorous a negation of Christian theistic structures.

Also, Hamilton confuses two meanings of the word "exist" when he distinguishes between atheists who never believe there ever was a God, and radicals who believe "there was once a time when having a god was appropriate, possible, even necessary." One use of "is" is ontological, the other is cultural and psychological. The experience of God and the reality of God must be distinguished.

II. *Theology in a New Key*

1. Dietrich Bonhoeffer, in E. Bethge, ed., *Letters and Papers from Prison* (rev. ed., The Macmillan Company, 1967), p. 188.

2. *Ibid.*, p. 195.

3. *Ibid.*, p. 196.

4. See Mack B. Stokes, "The New Quest for a Credible Theism," *Religion in Life*, Vol. XXXVII, No. 4 (Winter, 1968), pp. 572 ff.

5. John A. T. Robinson, *Honest to God* (The Westminster Press, 1963), p. 66.

6. *Ibid.*, p. 134.

7. *Ibid.*, p. 101.

8. *Ibid.*, p. 10.

9. Harvey Cox, *The Secular City* (The Macmillan Company, 1965), p. 3.

10. *Ibid.*

11. See Joseph Fletcher, *Moral Responsibility* (The Westminster Press, 1967).

12. Joseph Fletcher, "Reflection and Reply," in Harvey Cox, ed., *The Situation Ethics Debate* (The Westminster Press, 1968), p. 249.

13. See James Hillman, "The Language of Psychology and the Speech of the Soul," *Art International*, Vol. XIV, No. 1 (Jan., 1970).

14. John Charles Cooper, *Radical Christianity and Its Sources* (The Westminster Press, 1968), pp. 130–131.

15. Hamilton, "American Theology, Radicalism and the Death of God," in Altizer and Hamilton, eds., *Radical Theology*, p. 5.

16. *Ibid.*

17. Gabriel Vahanian, *The Death of God* (George Braziller, Inc., 1964), p. 246.

18. Paul van Buren, *The Secular Meaning of the Gospel* (The Macmillan Company, 1963), p. 100.

19. Hamilton, "The Death of God Theologies Today," in Altizer and Hamilton, eds., *Radical Theology*, p. 40.

20. *Ibid.*, p. 37.

21. Richard Rubenstein, "The 'Nothingness' of God," *The Christian Century*, Vol. LXXXV, No. 8 (Feb. 21, 1968), p. 231.

22. Richard Rubenstein, *After Auschwitz* (The Bobbs-Merrill Company, Inc., 1966), p. 257.

23. Thomas J. J. Altizer, quoted in Lee E. Dirks, "The Ferment in Protestant Thought," *The National Observer*, Jan. 31, 1966.

24. John J. Vincent, *The Secular Christ* (Abingdon Press, 1968), pp. 229–230.

25. Altizer, *The Gospel of Christian Atheism*, p. 9.

26. Barnabas Ahern, "The Permanence of Tradition," in Gregory Baum, ed., *The Future of Belief Debate* (Herder & Herder, Inc., 1967), p. 22.

27. Leslie Dewart, *The Future of Belief* (Herder & Herder, Inc., 1966), p. 204.

28. *Ibid.*, p. 65.

29. *Ibid.* See Chapter VI.

30. Michael Novak, "What Experience Tells Us About Being," *National Catholic Reporter*, Feb. 19, 1969, p. 18.

31. *Ibid.*

32. Michael Novak, "The Absolute Future," in Martin Marty and Dean Peerman, eds., *New Theology No. 5* (The Macmillan Company, 1968), p. 210.

33. *Ibid.*

34. Michael Novak, *A Theology for Radical Politics* (Herder & Herder, Inc., 1969), p. 120.

35. Michael Novak, "What Is Theology's Standpoint?" *Theology Today*, Vol. XXV, No. 1 (April, 1968), p. 39.

36. Michael Novak, "The New Relativism in American Theology," in Donald R. Cutler, ed., *The Religious Situation: 1968* (Beacon Press, Inc., 1968), p. 213.

37. Paul Peachey, "New Ethical Possibility: The Task of 'Post-Christendom' Ethics," in Martin Marty and Dean Peerman, eds., *New Theology No. 3* (The Macmillan Company, 1965), p. 103.

38. Gilkey, "The God Is Dead Theology and the Possibility of God Language," p. 14.

39. Albert Schweitzer, *The Teaching of Reverence for Life*, tr.

by Richard and Clare Winston (Holt, Rinehart and Winston, Inc., 1965), p. 35.

III. *Beyond Theism*

1. This brief reference to Spinoza is not entirely incidental, for I agree in part with Kraus: "So if Schweitzer were to acknowledge any of the philosophers as his guides it would not be Kant, but Leibniz and Spinoza." (Kraus, *Albert Schweitzer*, p. 73.)

2. Albert Schweitzer, *The Philosophy of Civilization*, tr. by C. T. Campion (The Macmillan Company, 1949), p. 304.

3. See Ian Ramsey, *Religious Language* (The Macmillan Company, 1957); also, "Contemporary Philosophy and the Christian Faith," *Religious Studies*, Vol. I, No. 1 (1965).

4. Paul Tillich, *The Protestant Era* (The University of Chicago Press, 1948), pp. xiv–xv.

5. Hamilton, "Questions and Answers on the Radical Theology," in Ice and Carey, eds., *The Death of God Debate*, p. 218.

6. *Ibid.*

7. Vahanian, *The Death of God*, p. 246.

8. Schubert M. Ogden, *The Reality of God, and Other Essays* (Harper & Row, Publishers, Inc., 1966), p. 19.

9. Harvey Cox, "Death of God and the Future of Theology," in Miller, ed., *New Christianity*, p. 381.

10. *Ibid.*, p. 388.

11. *Ibid.*, p. 389.

12. Kraus, *Albert Schweitzer*, p. 73.

13. Albert Schweitzer, *Kultur und Ethik* (Munich: Biederstein Verlag, 1948), p. 211.

14. *Ibid.*, p. 237.

15. Kraus, *Albert Schweitzer*, p. 42.

16. Clark, *Ethical Mysticism*, p. 159.

17. Kraus, *Albert Schweitzer*.

18. A strong sentiment shared by Richard Rubenstein whose whole theological shift away from the belief in the Jewish God of history and justice stems from the events surrounding the concentration camps. See his *After Auschwitz*.

19. Cousins, *Dr. Schweitzer of Lambaréné*, pp. 190–191. Italics mine.

20. Kraus, *Albert Schweitzer*, p. 43.

21. Schweitzer, "Religion in Modern Civilization," *The Christian Century*, Nov. 28, 1934, p. 1520.

22. Schweitzer, *Civilization*, p. 63.

23. Schweitzer, *Life and Thought*, p. 240.

24. See Paul Tillich, *The Courage to Be* (Yale University Press, 1952), concluding chapter.

25. Schweitzer, *Civilization*, p. 72.

26. *Ibid.*, p. 54.

27. *Ibid.*

28. *Ibid.*, p. 53.

29. Schweitzer, *Life and Thought*, p. 222. Italics mine.

30. Schweitzer, *Civilization*, p. 55.

31. *Ibid.*, p. 54.

32. See Michael Polanyi, "The Logic of Tacit Inference," *Philosophy: Journal of the Royal Institute of Philosophy*, Vol. XLI, No. 155 (Jan., 1966); also, "On the Modern Mind," *Encounter*, Vol. XXIV, No. 5 (May, 1965), p. 12.

33. See Paul Tillich, *Systematic Theology* (The University of Chicago Press, 1957), Vol. I, pp. 97–100.

34. See Michael Novak, *Belief and Unbelief*, pp. 51 ff.

35. See John Wild, "The Exploration of the Life-World," *Proceedings and Addresses of the American Philosophical Association* (The Antioch Press, 1961), Vol. XXXIV, Oct., 1961.

36. Carl von Weizsäcker, *History of Nature* (The University of Chicago Press, 1949), p. 190.

37. Albert Schweitzer, *Indian Thought and Its Development* (Henry Holt & Company, Inc., 1936), p. 1.

38. Schweitzer, *Life and Thought*, p. 150.

39. *Ibid.*, p. 153.

40. Schweitzer, *Civilization*, p. 59.

41. Schweitzer, *Life and Thought*, p. 150.

42. *Ibid.*, p. 153.

43. Thomas J. J. Altizer, quoted in William Braden, *The Private Sea* (Quadrangle Books, Inc., 1967), p. 178.

44. C. T. Campion, who translated *The Philosophy of Civilization*, found it more accurate, nine years later, to interpret it as "world-view," having first allowed the book to go to print with the word translated as "theory of the universe."

45. Kraus, *Albert Schweitzer*, p. 37.

46. Julius S. Bixler, "Productive Tensions in the Work of Albert Schweitzer," in A. A. Roback, ed., *Albert Schweitzer Jubilee Book*, p. 73.

47. Schweitzer, *Civilization*, p. 276.

48. Novak, "What Is Theology's Standpoint?" *Theology Today*, April, 1968, p. 39.

49. Schweitzer, *Civilization*, p. 279.

50. Novak, *Belief and Unbelief*, p. 172.

51. William Hamilton, *The New Essence of Christianity* (As-

sociation Press, 1966), p. 45.

52. Novak, *Belief and Unbelief*, p. 173.

53. Rubenstein, *After Auschwitz*, p. 82.

54. Schweitzer, *Civilization*, p. 76.

55. Kraus, *Albert Schweitzer*, p. 73.

56. Albert Schweitzer's letter written to me, July 7, 1952.

57. Schweitzer, *Civilization*, p. 77.

58. *Ibid.*, p. 274.

59. Everett, "Albert Schweitzer and Philosophy," *Social Research*, Winter, 1966, pp. 514–515.

60. *Ibid.*, p. 281.

61. *Ibid.*, p. 79.

62. *Ibid.*, p. 285.

63. *Ibid.*, pp. 278–279.

64. *Ibid.*, p. 280. Italics mine.

65. Schweitzer, *Life and Thought*, p. 158. Italics mine.

66. Schweitzer, *Civilization*, p. 278.

67. Kraus, *Albert Schweitzer*, p. 39.

68. *Ibid.*, pp. 39–40.

69. *Ibid.*, p. 40.

70. Schweitzer, *Civilization*, p. 302.

71. *Ibid.*

72. *Ibid.*, p. 303.

73. *Ibid.*, p. 304.

74. Schweitzer, "Religion in Modern Civilization," *The Christian Century*, Nov. 28, 1934, p. 1520.

75. Schweitzer, *Life and Thought*, p. 235.

76. Schweitzer, *Civilization*, p. 55.

77. *Ibid.*, p. 83.

78. *Ibid.*, p. 76. Italics mine.

79. John Middleton Murry, *The Challenge of Schweitzer* (London: Jason Press, 1948), p. 26; also see Kraus, *Albert Schweitzer*, p. 39.

80. Quoted from *The Humanist* (American Humanist Association, 1951), Vol. XI (Oct.–Nov., 1951), p. 197.

81. Tillich, *Systematic Theology*, Vol. I, p. 62.

82. Cox, "The Death of God and the Future of Theology," in Miller, ed., *The New Christianity*, p. 382.

83. It is strange that Altizer rejects Greek metaphysics and condemns it for misleading the church on the idea of the resurrection, etc., when the fundamental idea in Greek theology was that the Spirit first entered into union with human flesh (and the world) in the person of Jesus and thus gained the power to work upon man's

physical nature. This power of the immanent workings of the Spirit was further exercised among men *after* Jesus was separated from the world by his death and resurrection.

84. Schweitzer, *Civilization*, p. 73.

85. Clark, *Ethical Mysticism*, p. 143.

86. *Ibid.*, p. 142.

87. *Ibid.* See Ch. 18.

88. Hamilton, "Dietrich Bonhoeffer," in Altizer and Hamilton, eds., *Radical Theology*, p. 118.

89. Bonhoeffer, "Last Letters from a Nazi Prison," in Miller, ed., *The New Christianity*, pp. 293–294.

90. Schweitzer, *Civilization*, p. 305.

IV. *The Epiphany of Reverence for Life*

1. Schweitzer, *Life and Thought*, pp. 156–157.

2. P. G. Lindhart, in Langfeldt, *Albert Schweitzer*, p. 121.

3. Schweitzer, *Life and Thought*, p. 232.

4. Viktor E. Frankl, *From Death-Camp to Existentialism* (Beacon Press, Inc., 1959), p. 97.

5. Schweitzer, "The Ethic of Reverence for Life," in Clark, *Ethical Mysticism*, "Appendix I," pp. 182–183.

6. Schweitzer, *Civilization*, p. 210.

7. *Ibid.*, p. 239.

8. *Ibid.*, p. 212.

9. Albert Schweitzer, *Aus meinem Leben und Denken* (Hamburg: Richard Meiner Verlag, 1951), p. 137.

10. Schweitzer, *Kultur und Ethik*, p. 210.

11. *Ibid.*

12. *Ibid.*, p. 273.

13. *Ibid.*, p. 210.

14. *Ibid.*, p. 242.

15. *Ibid.*, p. 243.

16. Schweitzer, "The Ethics of Reverence for Life," *Christendom*, Vol. I, No. 2 (Winter, 1936), pp. 233–234. Published by The American Committee for the World Council of Churches.

17. Schweitzer, *Civilization*, p. 309.

18. *Ibid.*

19. *Ibid.*

20. *Ibid.*

21. Schweitzer, "The Ethics of Reverence for Life," *Christendom*, Winter, 1936, p. 227.

22. *Ibid.*, p. 282.

23. *Ibid.,* p. 283.

24. *Ibid.,* and Clark, *Ethical Mysticism,* p. 192.

25. *Ibid.,* p. 260.

26. Schweitzer, "The Ethics of Reverence for Life," *Christendom,* Winter, 1936, p. 239. Italics mine.

27. Murry, *The Challenge of Schweitzer,* pp. 11–12.

28. *Ibid.,* p. 13.

29. George Seaver, *Albert Schweitzer, A Vindication* (Beacon Press, Inc., 1951), p. 106.

30. Schweitzer, *Civilization,* p. xv. Italics mine.

31. Clark, *Ethical Mysticism,* p. 142.

32. Everett, "Albert Schweitzer and Philosophy," *Social Research,* Winter, 1966, pp. 529–530.

33. Schweitzer, Gifford Lectures, delivered at Edinburgh University, Nov., 1934. Mimeographed copy of the Edinburgh Newspaper Report, by the Albert Schweitzer Education Foundation, Chicago, Illinois.

34. Frankl, *From Death-Camp to Existentialism,* p. 97.

35. *Ibid.*

36. *Ibid.,* p. 99.

37. *Ibid.,* p. 101.

38. Schweitzer, "The Ethics of Reverence for Life," *Christendom,* Winter, 1936, p. 234.

39. Schweitzer, *Kultur und Ethik,* p. 218.

40. *Ibid.,* p. 237.

41. Schweitzer, *Civilization,* p. 209.

42. *Ibid.,* p. 210.

43. Schweitzer, *Kultur und Ethik,* p. 243.

44. *Ibid.,* p. 211.

45. Schweitzer, *Leben und Denken,* p. 206.

46. Schweitzer, *Civilization,* p. xv.

47. *Ibid.,* p. 281.

48. George Seaver, *Albert Schweitzer: The Man and His Mind* (Harper & Brothers, 1947), p. 342.

49. See Mircea Eliade, *The Sacred and Profane* (Harper Torchbooks, 1961), pp. 30–34, 52.

50. Clark, *Ethical Mysticism,* p. 142.

51. Schweitzer, *Civilization,* pp. 271 ff.

52. *Ibid.,* pp. 278 ff.

53. *Ibid.,* pp. 286 ff.

54. *Ibid.,* pp. 296 ff.

55. *Ibid.,* pp. 307 ff.

56. *Ibid.,* pp. 323 ff.

57. *Ibid.,* pp. 317 ff.

58. *Ibid.*, p. 287.
59. *Ibid.*, p. 289.
60. *Ibid.*, p. 291.
61. *Ibid.*, p. 314.
62. *Ibid.*, p. 309.
63. Thomas J. J. Altizer, "Death of God and the Uniqueness of Christianity," in Jerald C. Brauer, ed., *Essays in Divinity*, Vol. I, *The History of Religions* (The University of Chicago Press, 1968), p. 140.
64. Braden, *The Private Sea*, p. 171.
65. Martin Buber, *I and Thou*, tr. by R. G. Smith (Charles Scribner's Sons, 1958), p. 79.
66. *Ibid.*
67. *Ibid.*, p. 80.
68. Schweitzer, *Kultur und Ethik*, pp. 243–244.

V. *The Man Beside Others*

1. Robinson, *Honest to God*, p. 70.
2. Van Buren, *The Secular Meaning of the Gospel*. See Chapter VI.
3. See Gabriel Vahanian, *No Other God* (George Braziller, Inc., 1966).
4. See Altizer, *The Gospel of Christian Atheism*.
5. Altizer and Hamilton, eds., *Radical Theology*, p. xii.
6. *Ibid.*
7. Robinson, *Honest to God*, p. 76.
8. Cox, *The Secular City*, p. 112.
9. Novak, "What Is Theology's Standpoint?" *Theology Today*, April, 1968, pp. 37 ff.
10. See James M. Robinson, *A New Quest of the Historical Jesus* (London: SCM Press, Ltd., 1963).
11. See Jürgen Moltmann, *The Theology of Hope*, tr. by J. W. Leitch (Harper & Row, Publishers, Inc., 1967); also, Marty and Peerman, eds., *New Theology No. 5*.
12. Robinson, *Honest to God*, p. 76.
13. *Ibid.*
14. *Ibid.*, p. 83.
15. Jean Pierhal, *Albert Schweitzer: The Story of His Life* (Philosophical Library, Inc., 1957), p. 59. Italics mine.
16. Altizer, *The Gospel of Christian Atheism*, p. 25.
17. *Ibid.*
18. Albert Schweitzer, *The Quest of the Historical Jesus* (The Macmillan Company, 1950), p. 401.
19. Schweitzer, "Der Recht der Wahrhaftigkeit in der Re-

ligion," *Christliche Welt,* 1932, p. 941.
20. Schweitzer, *Quest,* p. 401.
21. Bowman, "From Schweitzer to Bultmann," *Theology Today,* July, 1954, p. 160.
22. Schweitzer, *Quest,* p. 403.
23. *Ibid.,* p. 401.
24. Cooper, *Radical Christianity and Its Sources,* p. 139.
25. *Ibid.*
26. *Ibid.,* pp. 139–140.
27. *Ibid.,* p. 140.
28. *Ibid.*
29. *Ibid.*
30. *Ibid.,* p. 141.
31. Schweitzer, *Life and Thought,* p. 232.
32. Schweitzer, *Civilization,* p. 106.
33. *Ibid.,* pp. 106–107.
34. *Ibid.,* p. 107.
35. *Ibid.*
36. *Ibid.* Italics mine.
37. *Ibid.,* p. 309.
38. Karl F. Reinhardt, *The Existentialist Revolt* (The Bruce Publishing Company, 1952), p. v.
39. Schweitzer, *Life and Thought,* p. 51.
40. Schweitzer, *Religions of the World,* p. 37.
41. *Ibid.,* p. 3.
42. Schweitzer, *Life and Thought,* p. 236.
43. Ulrich Neuenschwander, ed., *The Kingdom of God and Primitive Christianity,* tr. by L. A. Garrard (The Seabury Press, Inc., 1968), p. 98.
44. *Ibid.*
45. *Ibid.,* p. 99.
46. *Ibid.*
47. *Ibid.,* p. 158.
48. *Ibid.,* p. 159.
49. Schweitzer, "Appendix II," in Clark, *Ethical Mysticism,* concluding statement from the modified second edition of *The Quest,* p. 197.
50. Clark, *Ethical Mysticism,* p. 77.
51. *Ibid.,* p. 97.
52. Hamilton, *The New Essence of Christianity* (Association Press, 1961), p. 43.
53. Clark, *Ethical Mysticism,* p. 77.
54. Schweitzer, *Civilization,* p. 304.
55. Kraus, *Albert Schweitzer,* pp. 14–15.

56. Clark, *Ethical Mysticism*, p. 77.

57. Anyone desiring to know more graphically the difference between a Jesus and a Christ mysticism, I recommend read Altizer's most stimulating book *Descent Into Hell* (J. B. Lippincott Company, 1970) and contrast it with the last chapter of Schweitzer's *Philosophy of Civilization*. The differences will immediately become apparent, even though both of them are Radical theologians.

58. Mozley, *The Theology of Albert Schweitzer*, p. 113.

59. Seaver, *Christian Revolutionary*, p. 10.

60. Poem by George MacDonald, "That Holy Thing," in *The Story of Jesus in the World's Literature* (Creative Age Press, Inc., 1946), p. 25.

61. Hamilton, "The Shaping of a Radical Theology," *The Christian Century*, Oct. 6, 1965, p. 1221.

62. Clark, *Ethical Mysticism*, p. 81.

63. *Ibid.*, p. 80.

64. Several curious facts are worthy of note: Who was it Schweitzer said stood by his side as he labored building his jungle hospital? Jesus? No, it was *Goethe*. Who was it that came to his mind when the epiphany of Reverence for Life struck him? Jesus? No, it was *Buddha*. Whose picture did he have hanging above his bed in Lambaréné? Jesus'? No, it was *Darwin's*. Also, I am sure Schweitzer would be most unhappy if I omitted from this list the name of *Bach*, who had a great influence upon his life and who dominated so much of his energy, talent, and imagination.

65. Schweitzer, "Appendix II," in Clark, *Ethical Mysticism*, concluding statement from *Die Geschichte der Leben-Jesu-Forschung*, pp. 203–204. Italics mine.

66. Schweitzer, *Quest*, p. 403.

67. See Maynard Kaufman, "Post-Christian Aspects of the Radical Theology," in Altizer, ed., *Toward a New Christianity*, pp. 346 ff.

68. Altizer, "A Wager," in *ibid.*, pp. 304 ff.

69. Carl Braaten, Book Review: John McIntyre, *The Shape of Christology* (The Westminster Press, 1966), *Interpretation: Journal of Bible and Religion*, Vol. XXII, No. 2, p. 217.

VI. *The Phenomenology of Hope*

1. Cox, "Ernst Bloch and 'The Pull of the Future,'" in Marty and Peerman, eds., *New Theology No. 5*, pp. 195–196.

2. Albert Schweitzer, *The Mysticism of Paul the Apostle*, tr. by W. Montgomery (London: Adam & Charles Black, Ltd., 1931), p. 384.

3. *Ibid.*

4. Schweitzer, "The Conception of the Kingdom of God in the Transformation of Eschatology," in Mozley, *The Theology of Albert Schweitzer*, p. 114.

5. *Ibid.*, p. 88.

6. *Ibid.*, p. 92.

7. Schweitzer, *Mysticism*, p. 380.

8. Schweitzer, *Quest*, p. 402. Italics mine.

9. Schweitzer, *Kingdom of God*, p. 183.

10. *Ibid.*

11. *Ibid.*

12. Schweitzer, Epilogue, in Mozley, *The Theology of Albert Schweitzer*, p. 110.

13. Schweitzer, "Religion in Modern Civilization," in Seaver, *Albert Schweitzer: The Man and His Mind*, p. 338.

14. *Ibid.*, p. 337.

15. Schweitzer, *Quest*, p. 401. Italics mine.

16. *Ibid.* Italics mine.

17. Moltmann, *The Theology of Hope*, p. 37.

18. *Ibid.*, pp. 38, 39.

19. Schweitzer, *Quest*, p. 285.

20. William A. Beardslee, "The Motif of Fulfillment in the Eschatology of the Synoptic Gospels," in J. Coert Rylaarsdam, ed., *Transitions in Biblical Scholarship*, Vol. VI of Essays in Divinity (The University of Chicago Press, 1968).

21. *Ibid.*, p. 1.

22. Mozley, *The Theology of Albert Schweitzer*, p. 90.

23. *Ibid.*

24. *Ibid.*

25. Schweitzer, *Mysticism*, p. 384.

26. Schweitzer, *Religions of the World*, p. 13.

27. *Ibid.*

28. Schweitzer, *Civilization*, p. 290.

29. *Ibid.*, p. 291.

30. Schweitzer, *Quest*, p. 402.

31. *Ibid.*, pp. 402–403.

32. Schweitzer, *Civilization*, p. 284.

33. Schweitzer, "The Ethics of Reverence for Life," *Christendom*, Winter, 1936, p. 229.

34. Jürgen Moltmann, "What Is 'New' in Christianity: The Category of *Novum* in Christian Theology," in *Religion, Revolution, and the Future*, tr. by M. D. Meeks (Charles Scribner's Sons, 1969), p. 8.

35. *Ibid.*, p. 9.

36. Schweitzer, *Quest,* p. 399.

37. Schweitzer, *Mysticism,* p. 391.

38. Schweitzer, *Quest,* p. 254.

39. Seaver, *Albert Schweitzer: The Man and His Mind,* p. 228.

40. Introduction, in Marty and Peerman, eds., *New Theology No. 5,* p. 11.

41. *Ibid.,* p. 97. For an excellent discussion of Bloch's philosophy and its influence, see Francis Fiorenza, "Dialectic Theology and Hope, II" (Oct., 1968), and "III" (Jan., 1969), *The Heythrop Journal.*

42. Marty and Peerman, eds., *New Theology No. 5,* p. 96.

43. *Ibid.,* pp. 103–104.

44. *Ibid.,* p. 104.

45. *Ibid.,* p. 105.

46. *Ibid.,* p. 102.

47. *Ibid.,* pp. 86–87.

48. *Ibid.,* p. 107.

49. *Ibid.*

50. *Ibid.,* p. 108.

51. *Ibid.,* p. 109.

52. *Ibid.,* p. 87.

53. Schweitzer, "Religion in Modern Civilization," in Seaver, *Albert Schweitzer: The Man and His Mind,* p. 337.

54. Charles R. Joy, ed., *Albert Schweitzer: An Anthology* (Beacon Press, Inc., 1947), p. 215.

55. Schweitzer, *Religions of the World,* p. 26.

56. Schweitzer, "The Concept of the Kingdom of God," in Mozley, *The Theology of Albert Schweitzer,* p. 115.

57. Moltmann, *The Theology of Hope,* p. 25.

58. Schweitzer, *Religions of the World,* p. 76.

59. See Albert Schweitzer, *Peace or Atomic War?* (Henry Holt & Co., Inc., 1958).

60. Schweitzer, *Life and Thought,* p. 241.

61. Nathan A. Scott, Jr., "The Modest Optimism of Albert Camus," *The Christian Scholar,* Vol. XLII (Dec., 1959), p. 272.

VII. *Schweitzer and the Future of Belief*

1. Schweitzer, "Religion in Modern Civilization," in Seaver, *Albert Schweitzer: Man and His Mind,* p. 335.

2. *Ibid.*

3. *Ibid.,* p. 337.

4. *Ibid.*

5. Dewart, source unknown.

6. Kaufman, "Post-Christian Aspects of the Radical Theology," in Altizer, ed., *Toward a New Christianity*, p. 347.

7. *Ibid.*, p. 348.

8. *Ibid.*

9. *Ibid.*, p. 347.

10. *Ibid.*, p. 352.

11. *Ibid.*, p. 351.

12. *Ibid.*

13. *Ibid.*, p. 348.

14. See Charles Hartshorne, *The Logic of Perfection* (The Open Court Publishing Company, 1962), Ch. 3; also, for Hartshorne's "quarrel" with Schweitzer, see pp. 315–320.

14a. Clark, *Ethical Mysticism*, p. 171.

15. *Ibid.*, pp. 174–175. The quotations of Schweitzer cited by Clark may be found in *Life and Thought*, p. 121, and *Civilization*, p. 184, respectively; the quote of Whitehead is in Lucien Price, *The Dialogues of A. N. Whitehead* (Little, Brown and Company, 1954), p. 389.

16. Gabriel Fackre, "The Issue of Transcendence in the New Theology," in Martin Marty and Dean Peerman, eds., *New Theology No. 4* (The Macmillan Company, 1967), p. 178.

17. *Ibid.*

18. Kaufman, *loc. cit.*, p. 351.

19. *Ibid.*

20. *Ibid.*, p. 352.

21. *Ibid.*

22. *Ibid.*

23. Schweitzer, *Quest*, p. 397.

24. Kaufman, *loc. cit.*, p. 355. It is also interesting to note from Kaufman's article, the similarity of Berdyaev's vision of the "era of the Spirit" and Schweitzer's ethical mysticism which views all Life as ultimately One. " 'The era of the Spirit can be nothing but a revelation of a sense of community which is not merely social but also cosmic, not only a brotherhood of man, but a brotherhood of men with all cosmic life, with the whole creation.' " (Kaufman, *loc. cit.*, p. 359.)

25. Alex R. Vidler, *The Church in an Age of Revolution* (Pelican Book, Penguin Books, Inc., 1961), p. 273.

26. Deba Prasad Patnaik, "Albert Schweitzer and Indian Thought," in E. R. Hazemann, ed., *Albert Schweitzer: A Symposium* (University of Louisville, 1969).

27. Pierhal, *Albert Schweitzer*, p. 122. Italics mine.

28. Bonhoeffer, *Letters and Papers from Prison*, pp. 239–240.

DATE DUE

F			
FE 22 '78			
OC 29 '79			
GAYLORD			PRINTED IN U.S.A